Desert Data

Exploring Data Governance in the Middle East

By

Dr. Tosin Ekundayo, FOLDN

Dedication

To My Sister,

Monisola Soule

Foreword

When I first began my foray into the world of data, the Middle East was often viewed through a limited lens, overshadowed by global giants or overlooked due to misunderstood complexities. However, having engaged with the region first-hand, I've come to appreciate its nuanced tapestry — a blend of time-honoured traditions and ground-breaking innovations. This book, in its thoughtful exploration, brings to life that very tapestry.

The author takes us on a guided tour, navigating the dunes and oases of data governance in the Middle East. Each chapter presents a facet of the region's relationship with data, from the interplay of culture and policy to the practical challenges and successes within key economic sectors. What truly sets this book apart, however, is its deep-rooted understanding of the region's ethos. It doesn't merely present facts and figures; it tells a story, a human story of a region striving to carve its distinct identity in the digital age.

As global conversations increasingly revolve around data privacy, security, and governance, there's a pressing need to consider perspectives beyond the familiar western narratives. "Desert Data" fills this void, offering invaluable insights not just for professionals in the field, but for anyone keen to grasp the global intricacies of our data-driven world.

As you embark on this journey through the pages of "Desert Data," I encourage you to approach it with an open heart and a curious mind. Allow the stories, examples, and analyses to expand your horizons and challenge your preconceptions. In doing so, you'll not only gain a deeper understanding of data governance in the Middle East but also a renewed appreciation for the diverse tapestry of global data narratives.

To the future, where the wisdom of the past meets the possibilities of tomorrow.

Cheers,

Marcus

Acknowledgement

The journey of writing "Desert Data: Exploring Data Governance in the Middle East" has been an enlightening and rewarding experience, and it would not have been possible without the invaluable support and guidance of many.

Foremost, I wish to extend my heartfelt gratitude to Lincoln University, Malaysia. The faculty and research team have been instrumental in providing research guidance, ensuring the richness and depth of the content presented in this book. Their dedication, expertise, and commitment to academic excellence have been a constant source of inspiration throughout this journey.

I would also like to express my profound appreciation to Synergy University, Dubai for creating an enabling environment that fostered creativity, critical thinking, and intellectual growth. Their unwavering support, state-of-the-art facilities, and a community of scholars have greatly contributed to the essence of this book.

Lastly, to all those who provided encouragement, feedback, and shared their knowledge and experiences – your contributions have been the backbone of this work. It is with great humility and gratitude that I acknowledge the collective effort that made this book a reality.

Table of Contents

Preface

In the heart of the dunes, where tradition meets modernity, lies a region that has continually enthralled the world – the Middle East. Its rich tapestry of history, culture, and faith intersects dynamically with the ever-evolving digital landscape, sparking unique challenges and opportunities. As the digital age advances, the guardianship and administration of data have emerged as central themes, impacting every facet of our interconnected societies. "Desert Data: Exploring Data Governance in the Middle East" serves as a beacon, guiding readers through this intricate landscape.

The book you hold attempts to navigate the unique confluence of factors that shape the Middle Eastern perspective on data governance. Drawing from deep-rooted traditions while looking keenly towards a digitized future, the region presents a study in contrasts, making it a fascinating subject of exploration. As you delve into these pages, you will uncover the complexities of balancing age-old cultural and religious values with the exigencies of a globalized, data-driven world.

Each chapter is meticulously crafted to weave insights from various economic sectors, highlight the interplay of culture and geopolitics, and present real-world case studies that breathe life into theoretical constructs. We embark on a journey from the foundational principles of data governance to the region's current landscape, highlighting challenges, successes, and charting the path forward.

Beyond its academic and professional implications, this book is also an invitation: an invitation to engage with the Middle East's digital transformation critically, empathetically, and optimistically. Whether you are a data professional, a policymaker, a student, or simply a curious mind, this book aims to provide you with a nuanced understanding and a renewed appreciation for the intricacies of data governance in this unique region.

As we stand on the cusp of a new era, where artificial intelligence, blockchain, and other revolutionary technologies promise to redefine our relationship with data, it is crucial to understand the regional particularities that influence how societies interact with these innovations. Through "Desert Data," I hope to offer readers a compass – guiding, enlightening, and inspiring deeper engagement with the Middle East's data governance narrative.

Welcome to this journey, where the sands of time meet the waves of the digital revolution.

Part I

Foundations and Context

Chapter 1

Introduction

In today's rapidly evolving digital landscape, data has become the lifeblood of modern society. It drives our economies, informs our policies, and underpins the technologies that power our daily lives. As the world grows increasingly interconnected, the significance of effective data governance has risen to the forefront of conversations among governments, businesses, and individuals alike. The Middle East, a region steeped in history and tradition, has found itself at the crossroads of this global digital transformation, grappling with the challenges and opportunities that accompany this shift.

The Middle East's journey toward robust data governance is a story of innovation, adaptation, and resilience. As nations in the region work to diversify their economies and embrace the digital age, they must navigate a complex landscape of cultural, political, and technological factors that influence their approach to data management. This book aims to delve into the intricacies of data governance in the Middle East, shedding light on the unique factors that shape its development and the strategies employed by stakeholders to advance their data-driven agendas.

The importance of understanding and implementing effective data governance cannot be overstated. In an era where data breaches, cyberattacks, and privacy concerns dominate headlines, ensuring the protection and proper management of sensitive information has become a pressing concern for organizations and individuals alike. Data governance encompasses not only the policies, procedures, and standards that govern the handling of data, but also the underlying values and principles that guide the decision-making process. By examining the Middle Eastern context, this book will contribute to the broader discourse on data governance, providing valuable insights and lessons learned from a region undergoing significant digital transformation.

While the challenges facing data governance in the Middle East are substantial, so too are the opportunities. As the region invests in infrastructure, education, and technology, it is uniquely positioned to leverage the power of data to drive innovation, improve the lives of its citizens, and foster collaboration among nations. In order to realize this potential, however, stakeholders must work together to develop comprehensive and adaptive data governance frameworks that address the region's unique needs and circumstances. Through a combination of expert analysis, case studies, and practical recommendations, this book will provide readers with the knowledge and tools they need to understand and engage with the dynamic field of data governance in the Middle East.

To paint a complete picture of the Middle Eastern data governance landscape, it is essential to consider not only the technical and regulatory aspects, but also the cultural and historical factors that inform the region's approach to data. This book will explore the role of religion, tradition, and regional geopolitics in shaping attitudes towards data governance, providing readers with a holistic understanding of the forces at play. By acknowledging the region's rich history and diverse cultures, we can better appreciate the unique challenges and opportunities that the Middle East faces in its pursuit of effective data governance.

In the end, the story of data governance in the Middle East is one of possibility and promise. As nations across the region work to harness the power of data and leverage it for the benefit of their citizens, they have the potential to redefine the role of the Middle East in the global digital landscape. This book serves as a guide and a resource for those interested in understanding the complex and fascinating world of data governance in this vital and dynamic region.

Background on the Middle East region

The Middle East, a region known for its rich history, cultural diversity, and natural resources, has long been at the center of global geopolitics. Stretching from the eastern Mediterranean to the Arabian Peninsula and encompassing parts of North Africa, the Middle East is home to a tapestry of ethnicities, religions, and languages, each with its own unique customs and traditions. This complex socio-cultural landscape has influenced the region's approach to the digital age, and consequently, to data governance.

For centuries, the Middle East has been a crossroads for trade, culture, and ideas, making it a melting pot of influences from neighboring regions. This interconnectedness has been both an asset and a challenge, as it has fostered a wealth of cultural exchange, while also exposing the region to external forces, both political and economic. The Middle East's diverse cultural heritage, coupled with its strategic geopolitical position, has shaped the way its nations approach various aspects of modern life, including technology and data management. The region's economy has historically been driven by its abundant natural resources, most notably oil and natural gas. However, the Middle East has increasingly recognized the need to diversify its economic base, as the world shifts towards renewable energy sources and more sustainable practices. As a result, governments across the region have been investing heavily in infrastructure, education, and technology, aiming to create knowledge-based economies and capitalize on the opportunities presented by the digital age.

This commitment to digital transformation is exemplified by the region's ambitious development projects, such as Saudi Arabia's Vision 2030, the United Arab Emirates' Strategy for the Fourth Industrial Revolution, and

Qatar's National Vision 2030. These initiatives share a common goal: to harness the power of technology and innovation to drive economic growth, improve the quality of life, and enhance regional competitiveness on the global stage.

The case of the United Arab Emirates (UAE) serves as an illustrative example of the region's peculiarity when it comes to data governance. The UAE is a federation of seven emirates, each with its own distinctive cultural, social, and political characteristics. Despite these differences, the country has managed to establish itself as a regional hub for technology and innovation, attracting businesses, investors, and talent from around the world.

Central to the UAE's success has been its commitment to creating a supportive regulatory environment, one that fosters innovation while maintaining strict standards of data privacy and security. The country's data protection laws, such as the Dubai International Financial Centre's (DIFC) Data Protection Law and the Abu Dhabi Global Market's (ADGM) Data Protection Regulations, have been designed to align with international best practices, ensuring that businesses operating in the UAE can navigate the complexities of data governance with confidence. However, the UAE's approach to data governance is not without its challenges. The country's rapid development and diverse population have created a unique set of issues that must be addressed in order to maintain the integrity of its data governance frameworks. For instance, the UAE's expatriate population, which accounts for nearly 90% of its residents, introduces a range of cultural and linguistic factors that must be considered when implementing data policies and practices.

Moreover, the country must balance its desire for technological progress with the need to protect its citizens' privacy and adhere to cultural norms. This is particularly relevant in the context of emerging technologies, such as artificial intelligence and biometric data, which have the potential to revolutionize industries but also raise ethical concerns. Despite these challenges, the UAE's proactive approach to data governance has positioned it as a regional leader in this field. By adopting a holistic strategy that considers both the technical and cultural aspects of data management, the UAE has created an environment that encourages innovation while safeguarding the privacy and security of its residents.

The Middle East's dynamic socio-political landscape, along with its ongoing digital transformation efforts, makes it a fascinating region to study in the context of data governance. The interplay between tradition and modernity, coupled with the need to balance economic development and cultural preservation, has resulted in a unique set of challenges and opportunities for governments, businesses, and individuals alike. In countries like Israel, which boasts a thriving tech ecosystem and has earned the nickname "Silicon Wadi," data governance is crucial to maintaining its competitive edge in innovation. Israel's strong emphasis on research and development, bolstered by its robust academic institutions and defense sector, has led to a flourishing technology industry. The nation has managed to cultivate an environment that encourages the growth of start-ups and the exploration of cutting-edge technologies, all while navigating the intricacies of data governance within a complex geopolitical setting.

Similarly, countries like Iran, which face significant political and economic challenges, have sought to leverage the power of technology to improve the lives of their citizens and strengthen their economies. Despite being subject to international sanctions and having limited access to global markets, Iran has demonstrated remarkable resilience and ingenuity in developing its domestic technology sector. Data governance, in this context, becomes a critical tool for ensuring that the nation's burgeoning tech industry adheres to global standards and best practices, enabling it to overcome obstacles and foster a sustainable growth trajectory.

The region's ongoing efforts to modernize and diversify its economies have also given rise to numerous cross-border collaborations and data-sharing initiatives. One such example is the Arab Digital Economy Strategy, which aims to foster greater cooperation among Arab countries in the digital sphere, promoting the exchange of data, knowledge, and best practices. This initiative underscores the importance of developing robust data governance frameworks at a regional level, in order to facilitate seamless and secure information sharing between nations.

Overall, the Middle East presents a unique and complex environment for the study of data governance. By examining the region's diverse cultural, political, and economic contexts, we can gain valuable insights into the factors that influence its approach to data management, as well as the strategies employed by stakeholders to navigate this dynamic landscape. As the Middle East continues to embrace the digital age and capitalize on the transformative power of data, it is imperative that its nations develop comprehensive and adaptive data governance frameworks that address their unique needs and circumstances. By doing so, the region can harness the full potential of its digital future, fostering innovation, growth, and prosperity for generations to come.

Importance of data governance in the digital age
In the digital age, data has emerged as an invaluable asset, driving innovation and growth across a multitude of sectors. The ability to collect, analyze, and leverage vast amounts of information has transformed industries, redefined business models, and created new opportunities for economic development. Consequently, effective data governance has become crucial to ensure the responsible management and protection of data. By examining data governance from a multi-sectorial economic perspective, we can better understand its significance and the implications

of its application during unprecedented events, such as the COVID-19 pandemic.

Healthcare Sector

The COVID-19 pandemic has underscored the critical role of data governance in the healthcare sector. As the world grappled with the outbreak, the need for accurate, timely, and secure data sharing became paramount in order to track the spread of the virus, develop effective treatments, and coordinate global public health responses.

Case Study: The World Health Organization (WHO) and COVID-19 Data

During the pandemic, the WHO played a pivotal role in collecting, analyzing, and disseminating COVID-19 data to inform public health policies and strategies worldwide. Effective data governance was crucial to ensure the accuracy, privacy, and security of sensitive health information shared across borders. By establishing clear data governance protocols, the WHO facilitated international cooperation, allowing countries to better understand the virus's behavior and make informed decisions to protect their citizens.

Financial Sector

The financial sector has been profoundly impacted by the digital revolution, with the emergence of fintech, cryptocurrencies, and online banking reshaping the industry. In this context, data governance plays a critical role in maintaining trust, ensuring compliance with regulations, and safeguarding sensitive financial data from fraud and cyberattacks.

Case Study: Financial Institutions and Remote Work during COVID-19

The pandemic forced many financial institutions to adopt remote work arrangements, increasing the reliance on digital tools and the need for robust data governance. Banks had to rapidly implement secure data management practices to protect customer information and maintain regulatory compliance while transitioning to remote operations. Proper data governance enabled financial institutions to navigate the challenges of remote work while continuing to provide essential services to their customers.

Retail Sector

The retail sector has witnessed a significant shift towards e-commerce, with online shopping becoming an integral part of consumer behavior. The effective use of data allows retailers to personalize marketing, optimize supply chains, and enhance customer experiences. In this context, data governance is vital to ensure the responsible and ethical use of consumer data, particularly regarding privacy and security concerns.

Case Study: Amazon's Response to COVID-19

The COVID-19 pandemic accelerated the adoption of e-commerce, with companies like Amazon experiencing unprecedented growth. Amazon leveraged its vast troves of customer data to respond to changing consumer needs during the pandemic, such as prioritizing essential items and implementing contactless delivery. By adhering to strict data governance standards, Amazon was able to utilize customer data to drive business decisions while maintaining customer trust.

The importance of data governance in the digital age is evident across various economic sectors. The COVID-19 pandemic highlighted the critical role of data governance in facilitating effective responses to unforeseen events while protecting privacy and ensuring security. By examining the applications of data governance in different sectors during the pandemic, we can gain valuable insights into the broader implications of data management and the significance of data governance in today's interconnected world.

Overview of the book's content and structure

The book's content and structure have been carefully designed to provide readers with a comprehensive understanding of data governance in the Middle East while offering practical insights and recommendations for navigating its complex landscape. By presenting a logical flow of topics, supported by relevant case studies and examples, the book aims to build a solid foundation of knowledge, enabling readers to effectively engage with the dynamic field of data governance in the region.

The book is divided into the following sections:

I. Introduction and Background

This section establishes the context for the book, providing an overview of the Middle East's rich history, cultural diversity, and unique socio-political landscape. It introduces the concept of data governance and its growing importance in the digital age. By exploring the region's journey towards digital transformation and economic diversification, readers will gain a holistic understanding of the factors that influence data governance in the Middle East.

II. Data Governance in Key Economic Sectors

To highlight the multi-dimensional nature of data governance, this section delves into its applications across various economic sectors, such as healthcare, finance, and retail. Each chapter will examine the unique challenges and opportunities that these sectors face in implementing effective data governance practices, supported by case studies from the COVID-19 era. This approach will allow readers to appreciate the nuances of data governance across different industries, as well as its broader implications for the region's economic development.

III. Cultural, Religious, and Geopolitical Factors

This section explores the role of culture, religion, and geopolitics in shaping data governance in the Middle East. By examining the interplay between these factors and data governance policies and practices, readers will gain valuable insights into the region's distinctive approach to data management. This section will also discuss the ethical considerations surrounding data governance, highlighting the importance of balancing technological progress with cultural and religious values.

IV. Regional Collaboration and Cross-Border Initiatives

Recognizing the potential for regional cooperation in the realm of data governance, this section examines various cross-border initiatives and collaborations that have emerged in the Middle East. By exploring the opportunities and challenges associated with these initiatives, readers will gain a deeper understanding of the importance of developing robust data governance frameworks at a regional level, and the role that such collaborations can play in fostering innovation and growth.

V. Best Practices and Recommendations

Building on the insights gleaned from previous sections, this part of the book will offer practical recommendations and best practices for implementing effective data governance in the Middle East. Drawing on case studies and expert analysis, this section will provide readers with actionable guidance on how to navigate the region's complex data governance landscape and contribute to its ongoing digital transformation.

VI. Conclusion and Future Prospects

The book concludes by synthesizing the key insights and lessons learned from the preceding chapters, highlighting the importance of data governance in the Middle East's journey towards a digital future. This section will also explore the potential implications of emerging technologies, such as artificial intelligence and blockchain, for data governance in the region, offering a glimpse into the future of data management in the Middle East.

By presenting a clear and logical structure, this book will enable readers to progressively build their understanding of data governance in the Middle East, appreciating its nuances and complexities while gaining the knowledge and tools needed to effectively engage with this vital and dynamic field.

Chapter 2

The Building Blocks of Data Governance

The global data governance landscape consists of various models, principles, and best practices that have been developed and adopted by countries and organizations worldwide. These foundations serve as a valuable reference point for the Middle East, as the region continues to advance its digital transformation initiatives and strengthen its data governance frameworks.

Several key aspects of global data governance foundations are particularly relevant to the Middle East:

1. *Data Protection and Privacy:* As privacy concerns grow globally, countries have enacted legislation to safeguard personal data and grant individuals' greater control over its usage. The European Union's General Data Protection Regulation (GDPR) serves as a prime example of comprehensive privacy regulation that has influenced the development of data protection laws in the Middle East. Countries like the United Arab Emirates and Bahrain have introduced new data protection laws, drawing inspiration from the GDPR and other international standards.

2. *Data Security and Cybersecurity:* Ensuring the security and integrity of data is a top priority for countries and organizations worldwide. Global data governance foundations emphasize the need for robust

data security measures, including encryption, access controls, and regular security assessments. Middle Eastern nations have taken steps to strengthen their cybersecurity capabilities, recognizing the importance of securing critical data assets against growing cyber threats.

3. *Data Governance Frameworks and Best Practices:* A key aspect of global data governance foundations is the development and adoption of comprehensive frameworks and best practices. These frameworks often include principles such as data quality, data lineage, data cataloging, and data stewardship. By adopting and adapting these frameworks, Middle Eastern countries can establish robust and effective data governance practices suited to their specific needs and context.

4. *Cross-Border Data Sharing and Collaboration:* The interconnected nature of the digital economy has led to an increasing focus on cross-border data sharing and collaboration. Global data governance foundations recognize the importance of enabling secure and seamless data flows between countries, while also respecting national sovereignty and data protection standards. The Middle East can benefit from regional data-sharing initiatives like the Arab Digital Economy Strategy, which aims to promote cooperation and knowledge exchange in the digital sphere.

5. *Balancing Innovation and Regulation:* Global data governance foundations often emphasize the need to balance innovation and regulation. Striking the right balance ensures that data-driven innovation can flourish without compromising data privacy, security, and ethical considerations. This principle is particularly relevant for the Middle East, as the region seeks to foster a thriving digital economy while maintaining its cultural and religious values.

By examining global data governance foundations and their relevance to the Middle East, we can gain valuable insights into the strategies and best practices that can be applied in the region. As Middle Eastern countries continue to invest in digital transformation and data-driven innovation, adopting and adapting these global foundations will be crucial to ensuring responsible and effective data governance in the region.

To understand the intricacies of data governance, it is crucial to examine examples from around the world, offering a comparative and critical analysis of various case studies. By exploring how different countries and organizations approach data governance, we can appreciate its diverse applications and identify best practices that can be adapted to the Middle East context.

European Union: The General Data Protection Regulation (GDPR)

The GDPR, implemented in 2018, is a comprehensive data protection framework that has set a global benchmark for data governance. It grants individuals greater control over their personal data, mandates strict data security requirements, and imposes hefty fines for non-compliance. The GDPR has prompted many countries to adopt similar legislation and has influenced the development of data governance policies in the Middle East.

Case Study: GDPR Compliance Challenges

Despite the GDPR's success in establishing a harmonized data protection framework, it has not been without challenges. Many businesses have struggled to fully comply with the regulation, citing high costs and complexities associated with its implementation. Additionally, the GDPR's extraterritorial reach has sparked debates over jurisdiction and sovereignty in the digital realm. These challenges offer valuable lessons for the Middle East as it continues to develop its own data governance frameworks.

United States: Sector-Specific Data Governance

Unlike the European Union, the United States has opted for a sector-specific approach to data governance, with regulations such as the Health Insurance Portability and Accountability Act (HIPAA) for healthcare and the Gramm-Leach-Bliley Act (GLBA) for financial services. This approach allows for greater flexibility in addressing the unique needs of each sector but can also lead to fragmentation and inconsistency in data protection standards.

Case Study: The California Consumer Privacy Act (CCPA)

The CCPA, which came into effect in 2020, is a state-level data protection law that has been likened to the GDPR. It grants Californian consumers new rights concerning their personal data and requires businesses to adhere to strict transparency and accountability requirements. The CCPA's introduction highlights the growing demand for comprehensive data protection in the United States and offers a potential model for other states and countries to follow.

Singapore: The Personal Data Protection Act (PDPA)

The PDPA, enacted in 2012, is a key piece of legislation governing data protection in Singapore. It establishes a baseline standard for data governance, balancing the need for personal data protection with the desire to promote economic growth and innovation. The PDPA has been instrumental in positioning Singapore as a regional hub for data-driven industries, demonstrating the importance of data governance in attracting investment and talent.

Case Study: Singapore's Data Protection Trustmark (DPTM)

In 2018, Singapore launched the DPTM certification, a voluntary program that allows organizations to demonstrate their commitment to strong data governance practices. The DPTM helps to build trust among consumers and promotes a culture of accountability and transparency. This initiative highlights the role of voluntary schemes in complementing regulatory frameworks and could serve as a model for similar programs in the Middle East.

Analysing these global examples and case studies, we can gain a deeper understanding of the diverse approaches to data governance and the challenges and opportunities they present. This comparative analysis will inform the discussion of data governance in the Middle East, providing valuable insights and lessons that can be applied to the region's unique context.

Definition and principles of data governance

Data governance refers to the holistic management of data, encompassing its availability, usability, integrity, security, and privacy. It involves the development and implementation of policies, procedures, and best practices to ensure that data is effectively and ethically managed throughout its lifecycle.

The following are some key principles of data governance:

Data Quality

Ensuring the accuracy, consistency, and completeness of data is crucial for organizations to make informed decisions and maintain credibility.

Data quality management involves implementing processes and tools for data validation, cleansing, and enrichment.

Case Study: A multinational corporation faced significant financial losses due to poor data quality in its inventory management system. By implementing a comprehensive data quality management program, the company was able to rectify inconsistencies and improve its operational efficiency.

Data Security

Data governance requires robust security measures to protect sensitive data from unauthorized access, manipulation, or disclosure. Data security encompasses a range of practices, including encryption, access controls, and regular security assessments.

Case Study: A major healthcare provider experienced a data breach due to inadequate security measures, resulting in the exposure of patients' personal information. To mitigate future risks, the organization implemented a data governance framework that prioritized data security and privacy.

Data Privacy and Compliance

Adhering to data protection laws and regulations is a critical aspect of data governance. Organizations must ensure that they are compliant with relevant legislation, such as the GDPR or HIPAA, to avoid fines and maintain trust among stakeholders.

Case Study: A social media platform faced substantial fines and reputational damage for violating users' privacy rights under the GDPR.

The company subsequently introduced a data governance strategy that prioritized privacy and compliance to rebuild user trust.

Data Accessibility and Usability

Data governance ensures that data is easily accessible and usable by authorized individuals. This involves implementing metadata management, data cataloguing, and data lineage practices, as well as fostering a culture of data-driven decision-making.

Case Study: A financial institution struggled to gain insights from its vast troves of data due to poor accessibility and usability. By developing a data governance program that prioritized these aspects, the organization was able to streamline data access and improve decision-making.

Key components of effective data governance
Data Governance Framework

A well-defined data governance framework is essential for organizations to manage their data effectively. A comprehensive framework should include policies, procedures, roles, and responsibilities, as well as technical and organizational components.

Pointer: A global e-commerce company adopted a data governance framework that clearly outlined data stewardship roles, data quality standards, and security protocols. This framework allowed the company to scale its operations while maintaining data integrity and compliance.

Data Stewardship

Data stewards are responsible for ensuring the proper management and use of data within an organization. They act as liaisons between business and IT teams, facilitating communication and collaboration to address data-related challenges.

Pointer: A leading insurance company assigned data stewards to oversee data quality and compliance across different business units. These stewards played a crucial role in identifying and resolving data issues, improving overall data management.

Data Governance Tools and Technologies

The use of specialized tools and technologies is essential for effective data governance. These tools can assist in data cataloguing, lineage tracking, metadata management, data quality assessment, and security monitoring.

Pointer: A large manufacturing firm leveraged data governance tools to automate data cataloguing and lineage tracking, significantly reducing manual effort and improving data transparency.

Data Governance Maturity Assessment

Regular assessments of an organization's data governance maturity can help identify areas for improvement and track progress over time. These assessments often involve benchmarking against industry standards or best practices.

Pointer: A telecommunications company conducted a data governance maturity assessment to identify gaps in its data management practices. The assessment revealed areas for improvement, such as data quality and security, which the company then addressed through targeted initiatives.

Change Management and Communication

 Implementing data governance requires effective change management and communication strategies to ensure buy-in from stakeholders and foster a culture of data-driven decision-making. Clear communication of the benefits and goals of data governance is crucial to overcoming resistance and driving adoption.

Pointer: A retail organization successfully implemented a data governance program by engaging stakeholders at all levels through workshops, training sessions, and regular updates. This proactive communication approach helped build support and understanding for the initiative, leading to a smoother implementation process.

Continuous Monitoring and Improvement

Effective data governance involves continuous monitoring and improvement of data management practices. Organizations should regularly review their data governance processes, incorporating feedback from stakeholders and adjusting strategies as needed.

Pointer: An energy company established a data governance council that met quarterly to review data management practices and identify areas for improvement. This iterative approach enabled the company to adapt its data governance strategy in response to changing business needs and regulatory requirements.

Integration with Data Management and Analytics

Data governance should be integrated with an organization's broader data management and analytics initiatives. This ensures that governance practices are aligned with business objectives and that data insights are generated in a compliant and ethical manner.

Pointer: A pharmaceutical company integrated its data governance program with its data management and analytics initiatives, ensuring that data used for research and development was of high quality and adhered to regulatory requirements. This integration led to more reliable insights and faster decision-making.

By understanding the definition, principles, and key components of data governance, new industry players can develop and implement effective data governance strategies that align with their business objectives. Drawing from global case studies, organizations can learn from the experiences of others and tailor their approach to suit their unique context and requirements.

Global best practices and standards

Adopting global best practices and standards in data governance can help organizations achieve greater efficiency, ensure compliance with regulations, and foster a culture of data-driven decision-making. The following are some global best practices and standards that have contributed to the success of data governance initiatives:

Data Management Body of Knowledge (DMBOK)

The Data Management Association (DAMA) developed the DMBOK, a comprehensive framework for data management that covers various aspects of data governance, including data quality, data integration, and metadata management. By following the guidelines outlined in the

DMBOK, organizations can ensure their data governance initiatives are aligned with globally recognized best practices.

Case Study: A large financial institution adopted the DMBOK framework to guide its data governance efforts, resulting in improved data quality, streamlined data integration, and better collaboration between business and IT teams.

ISO 8000

ISO 8000 is an international standard for data quality management, providing guidelines for organizations to assess, measure, and improve the quality of their data. By adopting ISO 8000, organizations can ensure that their data governance initiatives prioritize data quality and are aligned with global standards.

Case Study: A global manufacturing company implemented ISO 8000 to improve the quality of its supply chain data, leading to more accurate forecasts, reduced inventory costs, and better supplier relationships.

COBIT (Control Objectives for Information and Related Technologies)

COBIT is a widely recognized IT governance framework that provides guidelines and best practices for managing IT resources, including data. Integrating COBIT into data governance initiatives can help organizations ensure that their data management practices are aligned with broader IT governance objectives.

Case Study: An insurance company implemented COBIT as part of its data governance strategy, leading to better alignment between data management and IT governance practices, improved data security, and more efficient use of IT resources.

ITIL (Information Technology Infrastructure Library)

ITIL is a set of best practices for IT service management that can be applied to data governance initiatives. Incorporating ITIL principles into data governance can help organizations ensure their data management practices are efficient, customer-focused, and aligned with business goals.

Case Study: A telecommunications provider adopted ITIL best practices for its data governance program, resulting in a more customer-centric approach to data management, better collaboration between IT and business teams, and improved service delivery.

GDPR and Privacy by Design

The GDPR has set a global benchmark for data protection, and its principles of Privacy by Design and Privacy by Default have become best practices for organizations worldwide. By incorporating these principles into their data governance strategies, organizations can ensure that data privacy and protection are ingrained in their data management practices from the outset.

Case Study: An e-commerce company integrated Privacy by Design principles into its data governance framework, ensuring that data privacy was a key consideration in the development of new systems and processes. This approach helped the company maintain compliance with the GDPR and build trust among its customers.

NESA Compliance

The United Arab Emirates' National Electronic Security Authority (NESA) has developed a set of regulatory standards and guidelines for the protection of critical information infrastructure, including data governance. By adhering to NESA's standards, organizations in the UAE can ensure that their data governance practices are aligned with national cybersecurity requirements.

Case Study: A leading bank in the UAE implemented NESA compliance as part of its data governance strategy, leading to enhanced data security, improved risk management, and increased trust from customers and regulators.

Saudi Arabia's National Data Management Framework (NDMF)

The NDMF provides guidelines and best practices for data management in Saudi Arabia, covering various aspects of data governance, including data classification, data protection, and data sharing. Adopting the NDMF can help organizations in Saudi Arabia ensure that their data governance initiatives are aligned with the nation's digital transformation goals.

Case Study: A major oil and gas company in Saudi Arabia adopted the NDMF to streamline its data management practices, resulting in improved data quality, better collaboration between business units, and more effective decision-making based on reliable data.

Dubai Data Initiative

The Dubai Data Initiative, launched by the Dubai Data Establishment, aims to make Dubai the world's smartest city by enabling the sharing and exchange of data between government entities and the private sector. By participating in the Dubai Data Initiative and adopting its best practices, organizations can ensure that their data governance efforts are aligned with the city's smart city vision and contribute to its digital transformation.

Case Study: A prominent real estate company in Dubai embraced the Dubai Data Initiative, sharing its data with government entities to improve urban planning and infrastructure development. This collaboration led to more efficient resource allocation and enhanced the overall quality of life in the city.

Data Localization and Sovereignty

In response to growing concerns around data privacy and security, some Middle Eastern countries have introduced data localization and sovereignty requirements, mandating that certain types of data be stored and processed within national borders. Adhering to these requirements is crucial for organizations operating in the region to ensure compliance and maintain trust among stakeholders.

Case Study: A multinational cloud service provider expanded its operations in the Middle East by opening data centers in several countries, including the UAE and Bahrain. By storing and processing data locally, the company was able to comply with data localization and sovereignty requirements, ensuring the continued trust of its customers and regulators.

By adopting these regional best practices and aligning with local standards, organizations in the World and Middle East can ensure that their data governance initiatives are tailored to the unique context of the region while remaining globally competitive. The success stories in these case studies demonstrate the potential benefits of adopting best practices and standards tailored to the Middle Eastern context, offering valuable insights for organizations seeking to strengthen their data governance initiatives in the region.

Chapter 3

The Historical and Cultural Fabric

Data governance is the management and protection of an organization's data assets to ensure accuracy, consistency, and security. The increasing reliance on digital technologies has placed data governance at the forefront of business concerns. In the Middle Eastern context, data governance is shaped by a unique combination of cultural and historical factors that influence how organizations in the region approach data management. Here, lets critically and comprehensively analyse these factors and their implications on data governance practices in the Middle East.

Cultural Factors

Collectivist Culture

Middle Eastern societies are generally characterized by collectivist cultures, where group identity and social harmony are highly valued. In such societies, people often prioritize the welfare of their group over their individual interests. This cultural trait impacts data governance by encouraging organizations to adopt a more collaborative approach to data management. However, it may also lead to reluctance in challenging established practices, potentially hindering the adoption of innovative data governance solutions.

Hierarchical Structures

Middle Eastern cultures often emphasize hierarchical structures, with clear distinctions between authority figures and subordinates. This can impact data governance by shaping the decision-making process within organizations. Decision-making in hierarchical cultures tends to be centralized, with authority figures assuming a significant role in determining data governance policies. While this approach can lead to clear lines of accountability, it might limit the participation of lower-level employees in the decision-making process, reducing the diversity of perspectives considered.

Trust and Relationships

Trust and relationships play an essential role in Middle Eastern cultures. Business transactions are often based on personal connections and a strong emphasis on trust. In the context of data governance, organizations in the region might prioritize working with vendors and partners with whom they have established relationships. This could potentially limit the range of solutions available to them, as well as their ability to adopt best practices from external sources.

Historical Factors

Legal and Regulatory Environment

The legal and regulatory environment in the Middle East has historically been less developed compared to Western countries. This has implications for data governance, as the region has often lacked comprehensive laws and regulations related to data protection and privacy. In recent years, however, countries like the United Arab Emirates and Saudi Arabia have introduced data protection laws, reflecting a growing awareness of the importance of data governance. Organizations in the region need to adapt to these changing regulations and ensure compliance with data protection laws.

Influence of Religion

Islam is the dominant religion in the Middle East, and its principles influence many aspects of society, including business practices. In the context of data governance, Islamic principles of honesty, transparency, and accountability can positively impact the way organizations manage their data. For instance, organizations may be more inclined to adopt transparent data governance practices to ensure ethical data handling. However, the interpretation and application of these principles may vary among organizations and individuals, leading to inconsistencies in data governance practices.

Legacy Systems and Infrastructure

Middle Eastern countries have historically lagged behind Western countries in terms of digital infrastructure and adoption of modern technology. As a result, many organizations in the region still rely on legacy systems and outdated data management practices. The transition to more effective data governance solutions can be challenging for these organizations, as they often face issues related to data silos, system integration, and employee resistance to change.

Data governance in the Middle Eastern context is shaped by a unique combination of cultural and historical factors. Understanding these factors is crucial for organizations in the region to develop effective data governance strategies that are sensitive to local cultural and historical nuances.

Recommendations for Data Governance in the Middle East

Given the unique cultural and historical factors that influence data governance in the Middle East, organizations operating in the region should consider the following recommendations to optimize their data governance practices:

1. *Encourage Collaboration and Innovation:* While respecting the importance of hierarchy and group identity, organizations should promote a culture that encourages collaboration and innovation in data governance. This can be achieved by involving employees from different levels and departments in the decision-making process, facilitating open communication, and providing opportunities for training and skill development.

2. *Adopt International Best Practices:* Middle Eastern organizations can benefit from adopting international best practices in data governance, such as the General Data Protection Regulation (GDPR) framework. By adhering to globally recognized standards, organizations can improve their data governance practices while fostering trust and credibility with international partners.

3. *Leverage Technology and Expertise:* To overcome the challenges posed by legacy systems and outdated data management practices, organizations should invest in modern technology and expertise. This can include the adoption of cloud-based solutions, data integration tools, and the hiring or training of skilled data professionals.

4. *Strengthen Legal and Regulatory Compliance:* As Middle Eastern countries continue to develop their data protection laws and regulations, organizations must ensure they stay updated on these changes and maintain compliance. This may involve appointing a

dedicated data protection officer or establishing a compliance team to monitor and manage regulatory requirements.

5. *Align Data Governance with Islamic Principles:* Organizations in the Middle East should align their data governance practices with Islamic principles of honesty, transparency, and accountability. By incorporating these principles into their data governance framework, organizations can foster ethical data handling and build trust with their stakeholders.

By addressing the unique cultural and historical factors that shape data governance in the Middle East, organizations can develop more effective data governance strategies that resonate with their specific context.

Cultural values and their impact on data governance

The Middle East is a culturally diverse region, with each country exhibiting unique cultural values that influence various aspects of society, including business practices and regulations. These cultural values play a significant role in shaping data governance practices and the adoption of data governance initiatives in the region. We will explore the unique cultural values present in the Middle East and discuss their implications on data governance practices and regulations.

Collectivism

One of the most prominent cultural values in the Middle East is collectivism, where group identity and social harmony are highly valued. Collectivism fosters a sense of shared responsibility among members of a group, which can positively impact data governance practices by promoting collaboration and teamwork. However, it can also create reluctance to challenge established practices and hinder innovation in data governance solutions, as individuals may prioritize group consensus over individual opinions.

The Implications: Organizations in the Middle East should strike a balance between maintaining group harmony and encouraging innovation. By fostering an environment that values open communication and collaboration, organizations can facilitate the adoption and implementation of data governance initiatives that cater to their specific needs.

Respect for Authority and Hierarchy

Middle Eastern cultures typically emphasize respect for authority and hierarchy. This cultural value impacts the decision-making process within organizations, with authority figures playing a significant role in determining data governance policies. While hierarchical decision-making can lead to clear lines of accountability, it might limit the involvement of lower-level employees in the decision-making process, potentially hindering the adoption of more effective data governance practices.

The Implications: To promote the adoption and implementation of data governance initiatives, organizations in the Middle East should consider involving employees from various levels and departments in the decision-making process. By encouraging diverse perspectives and fostering a culture of mutual respect, organizations can ensure the successful implementation of data governance policies.

Trust and Relationships

Trust and personal relationships are highly valued in Middle Eastern cultures, often influencing business transactions and collaborations. In the context of data governance, this cultural value can lead organizations to prioritize working with vendors and partners they trust, based on established relationships. While this approach can facilitate smoother implementation of data governance initiatives, it can also limit the range of solutions available and hinder the adoption of best practices from external sources.

The Implications: To optimize data governance practices, Middle Eastern organizations should be open to exploring new partnerships and solutions that align with their data governance needs, even if these solutions come from outside their trusted network. By prioritizing the adoption of effective data governance practices over personal relationships, organizations can better protect and manage their data assets.

Influence of Religion

Islam is the dominant religion in the Middle East, and its principles shape many aspects of society, including business practices. Islamic principles of honesty, transparency, and accountability can positively impact data governance practices by encouraging organizations to handle data ethically and responsibly. However, variations in the interpretation and application of these principles among organizations and individuals can lead to inconsistencies in data governance practices.

The Implications: Organizations in the Middle East should strive to align their data governance practices with Islamic principles while maintaining consistency and clarity in the implementation of these principles. By fostering a culture of ethical data handling, Middle Eastern organizations can improve their data governance practices and build trust with stakeholders.

The unique cultural values present in the Middle East significantly impact data governance practices and the adoption of data governance initiatives in the region. By understanding these cultural values and their implications, organizations in the Middle East can develop data governance strategies that respect and leverage these values, ensuring more effective and culturally sensitive data governance practices. This approach will enable organizations in the region to better protect and manage their valuable data assets in an increasingly digital and interconnected world.

Historical influences on the Middle Eastern approach to data

The Middle East, with its unique historical background, has experienced a different trajectory in the development of data management and protection practices compared to Western countries. Understanding the historical factors that have shaped the region's approach to data management is crucial for identifying the challenges and trends that impact the current state of data governance in the Middle East. This paper examines these historical influences and their contribution to the region's data governance landscape.

Historical Factors and Their Implications

Political Landscape and Government Priorities

The political landscape in the Middle East has historically been marked by instability, with ongoing conflicts and power struggles among countries in the region. As a result, governments have often prioritized national security and political stability over the development of data protection regulations and infrastructure. This historical focus on security concerns has contributed to a slower progression of data governance initiatives compared to more stable regions.

The Implications: The evolving political landscape in the Middle East presents both challenges and opportunities for the development of data governance practices. As governments increasingly recognize the importance of data protection and management, they can invest in strengthening the regulatory environment and infrastructure needed to support effective data governance.

Legacy Systems and Infrastructure

Middle Eastern countries have historically lagged behind Western countries in terms of digital infrastructure and the adoption of modern technology. Many organizations in the region still rely on legacy systems and outdated data management practices, posing significant challenges for data governance. The transition to more effective data governance solutions can be difficult, as organizations face issues related to data silos, system integration, and employee resistance to change.

The Implications: To address the challenges posed by legacy systems and infrastructure, Middle Eastern organizations need to invest in modern technology and expertise. Adopting cloud-based solutions, data integration tools, and training or hiring skilled data professionals can help facilitate the transition to more effective data governance practices.

Legal and Regulatory Environment

Historically, the legal and regulatory environment in the Middle East has been less developed compared to Western countries, particularly in the area of data protection and privacy. In recent years, however, countries like the United Arab Emirates and Saudi Arabia have introduced data protection laws, reflecting a growing awareness of the importance of data governance.

The Implications: As the legal and regulatory environment in the Middle East evolves, organizations in the region must adapt to these changes and ensure compliance with data protection laws. Strengthening legal and regulatory compliance is crucial for the development of effective data governance practices and the protection of individuals' privacy rights.

Education and Awareness

Historically, the Middle East has faced challenges related to education and awareness of data protection and management best practices. Limited access to quality education, particularly in the field of information technology and data management, has hindered the development of a skilled workforce capable of implementing effective data governance practices.

The Implications: Addressing the education and awareness gap is critical for the advancement of data governance in the Middle East. Governments and organizations should invest in capacity-building initiatives, such as training programs and educational resources, to improve understanding and implementation of data management and protection best practices.

The historical factors that have shaped the Middle Eastern approach to data management and protection continue to influence the region's data governance landscape. By addressing the challenges posed by the political landscape, legacy systems, the legal and regulatory environment, and education and awareness, the Middle East can make significant strides in the development and implementation of effective data governance practices. As the region continues to evolve and adapt to the digital age, a more robust and comprehensive approach to data governance will be essential for protecting and managing the valuable data assets of organizations and individuals alike.

Role of religion in shaping data governance attitudes

Religion, particularly Islam, plays a significant role in shaping various aspects of society in the Middle East, including business practices and attitudes towards data governance. Understanding the impact of religious beliefs on data governance is crucial for businesses and stakeholders operating in the region, as it provides valuable insights into the development of data governance frameworks, laws, and regulations. This paper investigates the influence of religious beliefs on data governance in the Middle East and discusses the potential implications for businesses and stakeholders.

Ethical Principles Derived from Religion

Islamic teachings emphasize ethical principles such as honesty, transparency, accountability, and respect for privacy, which can directly impact data governance attitudes and practices. For instance, the principles of transparency and accountability encourage organizations to adopt open and responsible data governance practices, which can lead to the protection of individuals' privacy rights and the responsible use of data.

Sharia Law and Data Governance

Sharia law, the moral and legal framework derived from Islamic teachings, can also influence data governance in the Middle East. Although Sharia law does not specifically address data protection or privacy, its principles can be applied to these areas. For example, the concept of amanah (trust) in Sharia law can be interpreted as the need to protect personal data entrusted to organizations. Similarly, the principle of maslahah (public interest) may encourage organizations to balance the use of data for business purposes with the protection of individuals' privacy rights.

Development of Laws and Regulations

The influence of religious beliefs on data governance can be observed in the development of laws and regulations in the Middle East. Several countries in the region, such as Saudi Arabia and the United Arab Emirates, have introduced data protection laws that reflect Islamic principles. For instance, the Saudi Data and Privacy Law emphasizes the importance of obtaining consent before collecting, processing, or disclosing personal data, which aligns with the Islamic principle of respecting individual privacy.

Implications for Businesses and Stakeholders

Alignment with Religious Principles

Businesses and stakeholders operating in the Middle East must ensure that their data governance practices align with religious principles to maintain credibility and trust with local partners and customers. This can involve incorporating Islamic principles such as honesty, transparency, and accountability into their data governance frameworks and fostering a culture of ethical data handling.

Compliance with Sharia-Influenced Laws and Regulations

As laws and regulations in the Middle East increasingly incorporate Sharia principles, businesses and stakeholders must adapt their data governance practices to ensure compliance with these rules. This may involve appointing a dedicated data protection officer, establishing a compliance team, or implementing data protection policies and procedures that reflect local regulations.

Cultural Sensitivity and Awareness

Understanding the impact of religious beliefs on data governance attitudes and practices is crucial for businesses and stakeholders to demonstrate cultural sensitivity and awareness when operating in the Middle East. By considering the influence of religion on data governance, organizations can better address the concerns and expectations of local partners, customers, and regulators, ultimately contributing to their success in the region.

Leveraging Religious Principles for Competitive Advantage

By aligning their data governance practices with religious principles, businesses and stakeholders can leverage these values as a competitive advantage in the Middle East. This approach can help organizations differentiate themselves from competitors, build trust with local partners and customers, and attract investments from stakeholders who prioritize ethical and responsible data handling.

Religious beliefs, particularly Islam, have a profound impact on data governance attitudes and practices in the Middle East. Businesses and stakeholders operating in the region must acknowledge and consider the influence of religion on the development of data governance frameworks, laws, and regulations to ensure their success in the region. By aligning their data governance

Part II

Regional Overview and Framework

Chapter 4

The Data Governance Landscape in the Middle East

Overview of data governance practices in the Middle East

The Middle East is a region characterized by diverse cultures, varying political landscapes, and complex legal frameworks, all of which play a significant role in shaping data governance practices. A comprehensive and critical analysis of the regional data governance landscape in the Middle East requires an understanding of the interplay of these factors and their impact on data privacy, security, and compliance.

One of the primary challenges in the Middle East's data governance landscape is the absence of a unified regulatory framework. Countries within the region have adopted different approaches to data protection, with some, such as the United Arab Emirates (UAE) and Saudi Arabia, enacting specific data protection laws, while others are yet to implement comprehensive regulations. This lack of uniformity in data protection laws and regulations can create complexities for businesses operating across the region, as they need to navigate multiple legal frameworks and comply with various standards.

The influence of cultural values on data governance practices in the Middle East cannot be understated. Cultural norms and expectations around privacy, data collection, and data sharing vary significantly between countries and can directly impact data governance practices within organizations. In many cases, businesses need to strike a delicate balance between respecting cultural values and meeting regulatory requirements. Trust is a crucial component of building effective data governance frameworks, and organizations that successfully address cultural concerns are better positioned to build trust with stakeholders. Political factors also play a significant role in shaping data governance practices in the Middle East. Political instability in certain countries can create uncertainties around regulatory enforcement, while government surveillance and data localization requirements can create additional challenges for businesses looking to ensure data security and privacy. Understanding the political landscape and its potential impact on data governance is essential for organizations operating in the region.

Despite these challenges, the Middle East presents numerous opportunities for businesses to develop and implement effective data governance practices. The growing demand for data-driven decision-making has led to an increased focus on data quality, privacy, and security. Many countries in the region are making efforts to develop data protection laws and regulations that align with global best practices, such as the European Union's General Data Protection Regulation (GDPR). This presents an opportunity for organizations to adopt a proactive approach to data governance and align their practices with international standards.

Moreover, the Middle East has witnessed a surge in investment in emerging technologies such as artificial intelligence (AI) and big data analytics. This presents opportunities for organizations to leverage these technologies in their data governance strategies, enhancing their capabilities to manage and secure data more effectively.

Country-specific profiles

The Middle East comprises diverse countries with distinct cultural, political, and legal environments, which influence their data governance practices and frameworks. This examination of data governance in various Middle Eastern countries highlights the unique approaches and challenges they face.

United Arab Emirates (UAE)

The UAE is among the leaders in the region when it comes to data governance. The country has implemented multiple legal frameworks to regulate data protection, such as the Dubai International Financial Centre (DIFC) Data Protection Law and the Abu Dhabi Global Market (ADGM) Data Protection Regulations. These regulations are largely aligned with international best practices, including the GDPR. However, challenges remain in terms of balancing data protection with the UAE's strong emphasis on national security and surveillance.

Saudi Arabia

Saudi Arabia has made significant strides in data governance in recent years, primarily driven by its Vision 2030 initiative, which aims to diversify the economy and promote digital transformation. The country's data protection landscape is governed by the Personal Data Protection Law (PDPL) and the Saudi National Cybersecurity Authority's Cybersecurity Law. While these regulations lay the foundation for robust data governance, businesses operating in Saudi Arabia may face challenges related to the lack of a dedicated data protection authority and stringent localization requirements for certain types of data.

Qatar

Qatar has implemented data protection regulations that focus on personal data privacy and security. The Qatari Personal Data Privacy Law (PDPL) is the primary legal framework governing data protection in the country. The PDPL emphasizes data security and the rights of individuals over their personal data, drawing inspiration from international best practices like the GDPR. However, the Qatari data protection landscape is still evolving, and businesses may face challenges in navigating the complex regulatory environment, which includes sector-specific regulations in addition to the PDPL.

Bahrain

Bahrain's data governance framework is based on the Personal Data Protection Law (PDPL), which aims to protect individuals' privacy and promote a safe digital environment. The Bahraini PDPL shares similarities with the GDPR and includes provisions on data subject rights, data security, and cross-border data transfers. Despite the PDPL's comprehensive nature, businesses operating in Bahrain may face challenges related to the law's relatively recent implementation and potential gaps in enforcement mechanisms.

Oman

Oman has not yet implemented a comprehensive data protection law. However, the country's Electronic Transactions Law and Cybersecurity Law address some aspects of data privacy and security. Oman's data governance landscape is characterized by a patchwork of sector-specific regulations, creating challenges for businesses in ensuring compliance with multiple legal frameworks. The absence of a unified data protection law may also make it difficult for organizations to adopt consistent data governance practices across their operations.

Jordan

Jordan's data governance landscape is governed by the Personal Data Protection Law (PDPL), which focuses on the protection of personal data and the rights of data subjects. The Jordanian PDPL includes provisions on data subject rights, data security, and data breach notifications. However, the law's relatively recent implementation means that businesses may face challenges in understanding and complying with its requirements. Additionally, the lack of a dedicated data protection authority in Jordan may complicate enforcement and regulatory guidance.

The Middle Eastern countries exhibit diverse approaches to data governance practices and frameworks, influenced by their unique cultural, political, and legal contexts. While some countries have implemented comprehensive data protection laws, others rely on sector-specific regulations or are in the process of developing data governance frameworks. Understanding the specific challenges and nuances of each country's data governance landscape is crucial for businesses operating in the region, as they strive to ensure data privacy, security, and compliance in a rapidly evolving digital landscape.

Comparisons with global benchmarks

To understand how the Middle East fares in terms of data governance compared to global benchmarks, it is essential to examine the region's practices in the context of effectiveness, compliance, and innovation. This comparison will help identify the strengths and weaknesses of the Middle Eastern data governance landscape and offer insights into areas requiring improvement.

Effectiveness

Effective data governance involves establishing a strong legal framework, promoting awareness and adoption of best practices, and ensuring robust enforcement mechanisms. In the Middle East, the effectiveness of data governance practices varies across countries.

Countries like the UAE and Saudi Arabia have taken significant steps to implement comprehensive data protection laws, such as the DIFC Data Protection Law and the Saudi Personal Data Protection Law (PDPL). These laws are largely aligned with global best practices like the European Union's General Data Protection Regulation (GDPR) and the California Consumer Privacy Act (CCPA). These countries have also established dedicated authorities to oversee data protection, such as the Dubai International Financial Centre Data Protection Commissioner and the Saudi National Cybersecurity Authority. However, other Middle Eastern countries, like Oman and Jordan, have yet to establish comprehensive data protection frameworks or dedicated data protection authorities. In these countries, data governance relies on a patchwork of sector-specific regulations, which may lead to inconsistent practices and weaker enforcement.

Compliance

Compliance with data governance regulations is crucial for ensuring data privacy, security, and responsible data management. The Middle East faces several challenges in this regard. The region's complex political landscape and varying degrees of legal enforcement may hinder consistent compliance across countries. Additionally, the lack of harmonized data protection regulations across the region can create complexities for businesses operating in multiple Middle Eastern countries.

Some Middle Eastern countries have adopted stringent data localization requirements, such as Saudi Arabia, which mandates that certain types of data must be stored within the country. These localization requirements may pose challenges for businesses in terms of compliance and operational costs, particularly for multinational corporations with cross-border data flows. Compared to global benchmarks, Middle Eastern countries are at different stages of compliance. Countries with comprehensive data protection laws and dedicated authorities, like the UAE and Saudi Arabia, are more likely to achieve higher levels of compliance than those without a unified legal framework.

Innovation

Innovation is crucial for advancing data governance practices and ensuring that they keep pace with the rapidly evolving digital landscape. Middle Eastern countries have made considerable strides in adopting innovative approaches to data governance.

The UAE, for example, has positioned itself as a regional leader in digital transformation, with initiatives such as the Dubai Smart City project and the UAE Artificial Intelligence Strategy 2031. These initiatives promote the development and adoption of cutting-edge technologies, including blockchain, artificial intelligence, and data analytics, which can help enhance data governance practices.

Other countries in the region, like Saudi Arabia and Bahrain, are also investing in digital transformation initiatives and fostering innovation through the establishment of technology hubs, such as NEOM in Saudi Arabia and Bahrain FinTech Bay. These efforts aim to create a conducive environment for the development of innovative data governance solutions. Despite these advancements, the Middle East still faces challenges in fully embracing innovative data governance practices, particularly in countries with less-developed digital infrastructures and fragmented regulatory frameworks. The region also grapples with issues such as a lack of technical expertise and limited access to advanced technologies, which may hinder the rapid adoption of innovative data governance solutions.

In comparison to global benchmarks, the Middle East exhibits a diverse landscape in terms of innovation in data governance. While countries like the UAE and Saudi Arabia are making significant strides in adopting innovative technologies and practices, other countries in the region are lagging behind due to various factors, such as limited resources, lack of expertise, and inadequate digital infrastructure. The Middle Eastern data governance landscape presents a mixed picture when compared to global benchmarks. Countries such as the UAE and Saudi Arabia have made significant progress in establishing comprehensive data protection laws, fostering innovation, and promoting compliance. However, other countries in the region face challenges in implementing effective and innovative data governance practices due to fragmented legal frameworks, limited resources, and varying levels of digital maturity. To enhance the region's data governance landscape and align it more closely with global benchmarks, Middle Eastern countries should focus on developing harmonized legal frameworks, investing in digital infrastructure, promoting cross-border cooperation, and fostering innovation. By addressing these challenges, the Middle East can strengthen its data governance practices, ensuring the protection of personal data, promoting responsible data management, and supporting the region's continued digital transformation.

Chapter 5:

Regulatory Foundations and International Collaborations

Regulatory environment and data protection laws

Key legislation and guidelines

The Middle East has been making significant strides in developing and implementing data protection laws and guidelines to ensure the privacy, security, and compliance of data within the region. As businesses and stakeholders increasingly rely on data-driven solutions, understanding the key data protection laws and guidelines in the Middle East becomes crucial. This analysis will discuss the major data protection regulations in the region and their implications for businesses and stakeholders.

UAE Data Protection Law

The United Arab Emirates (UAE) has been a regional leader in data protection legislation. In 2020, Dubai International Financial Centre (DIFC) introduced the Data Protection Law (DPL), which was heavily influenced by the European Union's General Data Protection Regulation (GDPR). The DPL aims to enhance data protection standards, ensuring that businesses operating in the DIFC adhere to strict data protection and privacy rules. Businesses operating in the DIFC are required to comply with the DPL, which includes implementing appropriate data protection measures, appointing a Data Protection Officer (DPO), and notifying the Commissioner of Data Protection about any data breaches. Non-compliance can result in hefty fines and reputational damage.

Saudi Arabia's Personal Data Protection Law (PDPL)

In 2021, Saudi Arabia enacted the Personal Data Protection Law (PDPL), which aims to regulate the processing of personal data and protect individuals' privacy. The PDPL, similar to the GDPR, outlines the rights of data subjects, the obligations of data controllers and processors, and the penalties for non-compliance. Businesses operating in Saudi Arabia must comply with the PDPL by obtaining valid consent from data subjects, implementing appropriate data protection measures, appointing a DPO, and reporting data breaches to the relevant authority. Non-compliance may result in severe penalties, including fines, imprisonment, or both.

Qatar's Data Privacy Law

Qatar enacted its Data Privacy Law in 2016, which regulates the processing, storage, and transfer of personal data. The law emphasizes the importance of obtaining explicit consent from data subjects and ensuring data confidentiality and integrity. Businesses operating in Qatar are required to comply with the Data Privacy Law by implementing suitable data protection measures, obtaining consent from data subjects, and reporting data breaches to the relevant authority. Non-compliance can lead to substantial fines and reputational damage.

Bahrain's Personal Data Protection Law (PDPL)

Bahrain's PDPL, enacted in 2018, is another comprehensive data protection law in the Middle East. The law outlines the rights of data subjects, the obligations of data controllers and processors, and the penalties for non-compliance. Companies operating in Bahrain must comply with the PDPL by implementing appropriate data protection measures, obtaining consent from data subjects, appointing a DPO, and reporting data breaches to the relevant authority. Non-compliance may result in substantial fines and other penalties.

Guidelines and Regulations in Other Middle Eastern Countries

While several countries in the Middle East have yet to enact comprehensive data protection laws, some have implemented guidelines and sector-specific regulations. For instance, Oman has issued data protection guidelines, while Kuwait has implemented data protection regulations within the banking sector. Businesses operating in Middle Eastern countries without comprehensive data protection laws should still adhere to any existing guidelines and sector-specific regulations. Additionally, organizations should proactively prepare for the potential enactment of more comprehensive data protection laws in the future.

The Middle East's evolving data protection landscape presents various implications for businesses and stakeholders operating in the region. Adhering to the key data protection laws and guidelines is crucial for maintaining compliance, avoiding penalties, and fostering trust with consumers and partners. As data protection regulations continue to develop in the region, businesses must remain vigilant and adapt their data governance practices accordingly.

International data-sharing agreements

As a data governance PhD holder, I understand that international data-sharing agreements play a crucial role in shaping the global data governance landscape. These agreements, which involve Middle Eastern countries, have significant implications on cross-border data flows and data governance within the region. In this analysis, we will explore the key international data-sharing agreements involving Middle Eastern countries and discuss their impact on data governance practices.

EU-GCC Cooperation Agreement

The European Union (EU) and the Gulf Cooperation Council (GCC) have established a cooperation agreement that includes provisions on the sharing of data between the EU and GCC countries, including Saudi Arabia, the United Arab Emirates, Qatar, Oman, Kuwait, and Bahrain. The agreement aims to facilitate economic and technical cooperation, promote the exchange of information, and enhance collaboration in various sectors. This agreement fosters a collaborative environment that facilitates cross-border data flows and encourages the adoption of data governance best practices between the EU and the Middle East. However, given the differences in data protection regulations, such as the EU's GDPR and the data protection laws in GCC countries, businesses must carefully navigate these complex legal frameworks to ensure compliance with all relevant regulations.

The Convention on Cybercrime (Budapest Convention)

Several Middle Eastern countries, such as Turkey, Israel, and Jordan, have signed or ratified the Convention on Cybercrime, also known as the Budapest Convention. The convention aims to promote international cooperation in combating cybercrime by establishing guidelines for data sharing and collaboration between countries. The Budapest Convention has facilitated cross-border data sharing and law enforcement cooperation in the Middle East. However, the convention's provisions on data sharing and privacy have raised concerns about potential conflicts with national data protection laws. As a result, businesses and stakeholders must be vigilant in ensuring their data governance practices align with both the convention's provisions and local data protection regulations.

Cross-Border Data Sharing in the Financial Sector

Several international agreements govern cross-border data sharing in the financial sector, such as the Foreign Account Tax Compliance Act (FATCA) and the Common Reporting Standard (CRS). These agreements require financial institutions in participating countries, including Middle Eastern countries, to share financial account information with foreign tax authorities to combat tax evasion and money laundering. These international agreements have necessitated the implementation of stringent data governance practices within the financial sector in the Middle East. Financial institutions must ensure compliance with various data protection regulations while adhering to the requirements of FATCA and CRS. This may require the development of robust data management systems and processes to support cross-border data sharing while maintaining data privacy and security.

Bilateral Data Sharing Agreements

Middle Eastern countries have also established bilateral data sharing agreements with various countries worldwide. These agreements typically focus on specific sectors or policy areas, such as law enforcement, counter-terrorism, or trade facilitation. For instance, the United Arab Emirates has signed data sharing agreements with countries like India and the United States to facilitate cooperation in areas such as law enforcement, security, and trade. Bilateral data sharing agreements can significantly impact data governance practices in the Middle East, as businesses and stakeholders must navigate the requirements of multiple international agreements. Ensuring compliance with these agreements and local data protection laws can be challenging, requiring a nuanced understanding of the various regulatory frameworks and their implications on data governance practices.

International data-sharing agreements involving Middle Eastern countries play a critical role in shaping the regional data governance landscape. These agreements have direct implications on cross-border data flows and data governance practices, requiring businesses and stakeholders to navigate a complex web of legal frameworks and compliance requirements. As the importance of data continues to grow globally, the need for robust and adaptable data governance practices in the Middle East is essential to fostering trust, collaboration, and innovation across borders.

Chapter 6

Stakeholder Engagement in Data Governance

Public and private sector involvement
Government initiatives and policies

As a data governance professional, I recognize the critical role that Middle Eastern governments play in shaping data governance practices within the region. Governments in the Middle East have implemented various initiatives and policies to promote data protection, security, and compliance, reflecting their commitment to creating a robust data governance ecosystem. In this examination, we will explore the actions taken by Middle Eastern governments to shape data governance practices and discuss the impact of these initiatives on businesses and stakeholders in the region.

Development of National Data Protection Laws

Middle Eastern countries have increasingly recognized the importance of data protection and have taken steps to develop national data protection laws. For instance, the United Arab Emirates (UAE) has introduced the Dubai International Financial Centre (DIFC) Data Protection Law and the Abu Dhabi Global Market (ADGM) Data Protection Regulations, which set out comprehensive data protection requirements for businesses operating within these jurisdictions. Similarly, Saudi Arabia has implemented the Personal Data Protection Law (PDPL), which governs the processing of personal data within the country. These national data protection laws have significantly influenced data governance practices in the Middle East by setting out clear requirements and guidelines for businesses operating in the region. Companies must ensure compliance with these regulations, which often necessitates the development of robust data governance frameworks, policies, and procedures.

Cybersecurity Regulations and Initiatives

In response to the growing threat of cyberattacks and data breaches, Middle Eastern governments have enacted various cybersecurity regulations and launched initiatives to strengthen data security. For example, Saudi Arabia has established the National Cybersecurity Authority (NCA), responsible for implementing the country's cybersecurity strategy and coordinating efforts to protect national infrastructure and data. Furthermore, the UAE has implemented the National Cybersecurity Strategy, which aims to create a safe and resilient digital ecosystem by enhancing cybersecurity measures across all sectors. The introduction of these cybersecurity regulations and initiatives has led businesses in the Middle East to place greater emphasis on data security within their data governance practices. Organizations must invest in robust cybersecurity measures and technologies to protect sensitive data and ensure compliance with government requirements.

Digital Transformation Initiatives

Middle Eastern governments have launched digital transformation initiatives aimed at modernizing their economies and leveraging technology to improve public services. For example, Saudi Arabia's Vision 2030 and the UAE's Vision 2021 both emphasize the importance of digital transformation in driving economic growth and improving public services. As part of these initiatives, governments have implemented measures to support data governance, including the establishment of data management frameworks and data-sharing platforms. Digital transformation initiatives have highlighted the need for effective data governance practices in the Middle East, as governments increasingly rely on data to make informed decisions and improve public services. Businesses operating in the region must adapt their data governance practices to align with government initiatives, ensuring that they are well-positioned to capitalize on the opportunities presented by digital transformation.

Data Localization and Cross-Border Data Flow Regulations

Middle Eastern governments have implemented data localization and cross-border data flow regulations to control the transfer and storage of sensitive data. For example, the UAE's DIFC Data Protection Law and ADGM Data Protection Regulations include data localization provisions that require certain types of data to be stored within the UAE. Similarly, the Saudi Arabian PDPL includes restrictions on the transfer of personal data outside the country. Data localization and cross-border data flow regulations have direct implications for data governance practices in the Middle East, as organizations must ensure that their data management processes comply with these requirements. This often necessitates the development of complex data storage and transfer solutions, which can impact the efficiency and cost-effectiveness of data governance practices.

Public-Private Partnerships and Collaboration

Middle Eastern governments have recognized the importance of collaborating with the private sector to promote effective data governance practices. Public-private partnerships (PPPs) have emerged as a vital instrument in achieving this goal, enabling governments and businesses to share knowledge, resources, and best practices. For instance, the UAE's Smart Dubai initiative has fostered partnerships between government entities and private organizations to develop and implement innovative data governance solutions. Public-private partnerships and collaboration have fostered a culture of innovation and knowledge-sharing in the Middle Eastern data governance landscape. Businesses operating in the region can benefit from these partnerships by gaining access to cutting-edge data governance technologies and best practices, enhancing their ability to protect sensitive data and maintain regulatory compliance.

Capacity Building and Education

Middle Eastern governments have also invested in capacity building and education initiatives to promote data governance expertise within the region. These efforts aim to develop a skilled workforce capable of managing the complex data governance challenges faced by businesses and stakeholders in the Middle East. For example, the UAE's National Program for Artificial Intelligence and the Saudi Data and Artificial Intelligence Authority (SDAIA) both include initiatives to train professionals in data governance, data science, and artificial intelligence. Capacity building and education initiatives have helped to create a skilled workforce of data governance professionals in the Middle East, enabling businesses and stakeholders to access the expertise they need to effectively manage their data governance practices. These initiatives have also fostered a culture of continuous learning and improvement, as organizations seek to stay up-to-date with the latest data governance trends and best practices.

Regional Cooperation and Harmonization

Middle Eastern governments have increasingly recognized the need for regional cooperation and harmonization in data governance practices. This has led to the development of regional forums and initiatives aimed at promoting dialogue and cooperation between Middle Eastern countries on data governance issues. For example, the Arab League's Arab Digital Economy Strategy seeks to foster collaboration among member states in areas such as data protection, cybersecurity, and digital transformation. Regional cooperation and harmonization efforts have the potential to create a more unified data governance landscape in the Middle East, enabling businesses and stakeholders to navigate the region's complex regulatory environment more easily. These efforts can also promote the sharing of best practices and resources, enhancing the overall effectiveness of data governance practices in the region.

Middle Eastern governments have a significant influence on the regional data governance landscape through their initiatives and policies, which focus on promoting data protection, security, compliance, and collaboration. By understanding the role of governments in shaping data governance practices, businesses and stakeholders can better adapt their strategies to align with regional requirements and capitalize on the opportunities presented by the Middle Eastern data governance landscape.

Corporate strategies and best practices
Private sector organizations operating in the Middle East face a unique set of data governance challenges, given the region's complex regulatory

environment and cultural nuances. As a result, these organizations have adopted various data governance strategies and best practices to ensure data protection, privacy, and compliance. In this analysis, we will discuss the effectiveness of these strategies and their alignment with regional regulations and global standards.

Adoption of Data Governance Frameworks

To effectively manage their data governance challenges, private sector organizations in the Middle East have turned to internationally recognized data governance frameworks, such as COBIT, DAMA-DMBOK, and ITIL. These frameworks provide a structured approach to managing data governance processes and aligning them with organizational objectives. Adopting data governance frameworks helps organizations in the Middle East to establish clear data governance policies and procedures, which can improve data quality, security, and privacy. Moreover, by adhering to globally recognized frameworks, these organizations demonstrate their commitment to best practices and enhance their reputation among customers, partners, and regulators.

Data Privacy and Security by Design

Given the heightened focus on data protection and privacy in the Middle East, private sector organizations have increasingly adopted the principles of data privacy and security by design. This approach involves integrating data protection and security measures into the development of business processes, systems, and applications from the outset, rather than as an afterthought. By adopting data privacy and security by design, organizations can reduce the risk of data breaches and ensure compliance with regional data protection regulations. Additionally, this proactive approach can help organizations avoid costly penalties and reputational damage associated with data breaches.

Training and Awareness Programs

Private sector organizations in the Middle East have recognized the importance of employee training and awareness programs in promoting effective data governance practices. These programs help to create a culture of data privacy and security by educating employees on the importance of protecting sensitive data and their role in ensuring compliance with regional regulations. Employee training and awareness programs can significantly reduce the risk of human error, which is a leading cause of data breaches. By equipping employees with the knowledge and skills needed to handle sensitive data securely, organizations can better protect their data and maintain compliance with regional data protection laws.

Data Governance Audits and Assessments

To ensure the ongoing effectiveness of their data governance practices, private sector organizations in the Middle East have implemented regular data governance audits and assessments. These audits help organizations identify areas of non-compliance or potential risk and take corrective action to address any issues. Regular data governance audits and assessments enable organizations to monitor their data governance practices continuously and ensure alignment with regional regulations and global best practices. This proactive approach can help organizations avoid penalties and reputational damage associated with non-compliance.

Collaborative Approach to Data Governance

In the Middle East, private sector organizations have increasingly embraced a collaborative approach to data governance, working closely with government entities, industry associations, and other stakeholders to share best practices and resources. This collaboration allows organizations to stay informed about regulatory changes, technological advancements, and emerging trends in data governance. A collaborative approach to data governance enables organizations to learn from the experiences and expertise of others, ensuring that their data governance practices remain current and aligned with regional requirements and global best practices.

Private sector organizations in the Middle East have adopted a range of data governance strategies and best practices to navigate the region's complex regulatory landscape and protect sensitive data effectively. By embracing data governance frameworks, data privacy and security by design, employee training and awareness programs, regular audits and assessments, and collaborative initiatives, these organizations can ensure that their data governance practices align with regional regulations and global standards.

Part III

Challenges, Opportunities, and Success Stories

Chapter 7

Navigating Data Privacy and Security

In the heart of the Arabian desert, beneath the scorching sun and swirling sands, there exists a complex ecosystem of flora and fauna that thrives despite its harsh environment. This delicate balance of life is a testament to resilience, adaptation, and the ability to find opportunities in even the most challenging of circumstances. In a similar vein, the Middle East, a region steeped in rich history, culture, and natural resources, now faces the challenge of navigating the uncharted territory of data governance. Just as the desert ecosystem has evolved and adapted, so too must the Middle East rise to meet the unique challenges and opportunities that data governance presents.

We will embark on a journey to explore the nuances of data governance in the Middle Eastern context, examining the obstacles that stand in the way, and the potential pathways to overcoming them. As we traverse this landscape, we will uncover the ways in which the region can harness the power of data to unlock new opportunities and drive growth.

The Oasis of Data Governance

Data governance can be likened to an oasis in the desert: a vital source of sustenance and refuge that enables growth and prosperity in the surrounding landscape. In a modern, interconnected world, data governance is a critical element for countries to remain competitive and foster innovation. Effective data governance allows for the responsible, secure, and efficient management of information, creating a framework that supports data-driven decision-making and enhances transparency. However, the oasis of data governance is not without its challenges. Countries in the Middle East face a myriad of hurdles in their quest to establish robust data governance systems, ranging from regulatory gaps and fragmentation to cultural barriers and a lack of trust in data sharing. These challenges can be as formidable as the shifting sands and scorching heat of the desert, but by examining them in depth, we can begin to plot a course towards the oasis of opportunity that data governance represents.

The Shifting Sands of Regulation

One of the most significant challenges to data governance in the Middle East is the fragmented nature of regulations that govern data management, privacy, and security. In some countries, regulations are either non-existent or outdated, leaving a vacuum that breeds uncertainty and stifles innovation. In others, a patchwork of overlapping and sometimes contradictory regulations creates confusion and impedes progress. To navigate these shifting sands, Middle Eastern countries must establish clear, consistent, and comprehensive regulatory frameworks that align with international standards. This will not only provide a solid foundation for data governance but also enhance the region's credibility in the eyes of foreign investors and partners. Furthermore, harmonizing regulations across the region will facilitate cross-border data flows and foster greater collaboration, unlocking the potential for increased trade, economic integration, and technological innovation.

The Mirage of Trust

In the desert, a mirage is a tantalizing illusion that promises respite but often leads to disappointment and despair. Similarly, the lack of trust in data sharing and management is a formidable barrier to data governance in the Middle East. This mistrust stems from a variety of factors, including concerns about data privacy, security, and misuse, as well as a cultural reluctance to share information. To transform this mirage of trust into a tangible reality, Middle Eastern countries must invest in building strong data protection frameworks and robust cybersecurity infrastructure. Educating citizens about the benefits of data sharing and addressing concerns about privacy and security can help to create a culture of trust that supports data governance initiatives. Moreover, public-private partnerships can serve as a catalyst for collaboration, enabling the sharing of best practices, resources, and expertise to strengthen data governance efforts across the region.

The Scorching Heat of Capacity and Infrastructure

In the desert, the scorching heat can be an overwhelming obstacle to survival, sapping the strength and resilience of even the most hardened travelers. In the context of data governance, the scorching heat represents the challenges of capacity and infrastructure that the Middle East must overcome to fully realize the potential of data-driven innovation. Building a robust data governance ecosystem requires not only the development of physical infrastructure, such as data centers and high-speed connectivity, but also the cultivation of human capital to manage and analyze the data effectively. To mitigate the impact of this scorching heat, Middle Eastern countries must invest in developing their digital infrastructure, ensuring that it is resilient, secure, and scalable. This will involve collaborating with private sector stakeholders, leveraging their expertise and resources to build state-of-the-art data centers and expand broadband connectivity. In addition, fostering a culture of lifelong learning and investing in education and training programs that focus on data science, analytics, and related fields will help to bridge the skills gap and empower the region's workforce to thrive in a data-driven world.

The Winds of Change: Embracing Digital Transformation

The winds of change are blowing across the Middle Eastern desert, heralding the arrival of a new era of digital transformation. As governments and businesses in the region increasingly recognize the value of data as a strategic asset, they are beginning to embrace digital transformation and adopt innovative technologies such as artificial intelligence, machine learning, and the Internet of Things.

However, to fully harness the power of these technologies, Middle Eastern countries must address the challenges and seize the opportunities that data governance presents. By establishing comprehensive regulatory frameworks, building trust in data sharing, and investing in capacity and infrastructure, the region can create a fertile environment for data-driven innovation and growth.

The Oasis of Opportunity in the Middle East

As we reach the end of our journey through the challenges and opportunities of Middle Eastern data governance, it is clear that there is a vast and untapped potential waiting to be unlocked. By overcoming the obstacles that stand in their way, Middle Eastern countries can transform their data governance landscapes from barren deserts into thriving oases of opportunity. To achieve this, the region must continue to foster collaboration between governments, businesses, and other stakeholders, working together to create a shared vision for data governance that is both ambitious and achievable. This will involve not only addressing the immediate challenges but also anticipating future trends and developments, ensuring that the region remains agile and adaptive in the face of an ever-evolving global data landscape.

The Middle East stands at a critical juncture in its data governance journey. The challenges are formidable, but the opportunities are equally vast. By embracing the winds of change and adapting to the shifting sands of regulation, the region can create a data governance ecosystem that not only supports innovation and growth but also ensures the responsible, secure, and efficient management of its most valuable resource: data. Just as the desert ecosystem has thrived through resilience and adaptation, so too can the Middle East rise to meet the challenges and opportunities of data governance, unlocking a brighter, more prosperous future for all.

Data Privacy and Security Concerns in the Middle East

The Middle East, a region rich in culture and history, faces a new set of challenges in the digital age. As the world becomes increasingly interconnected and data-driven, the Middle Eastern countries must grapple with the complex issues of data privacy and security. These concerns are particularly acute in a region that is characterized by diverse political, social, and economic landscapes, making the task of establishing effective data protection mechanisms all the more challenging.

The Importance of Data Privacy and Security

In today's digital world, data privacy and security are fundamental components of effective data governance. Ensuring the protection of personal and sensitive information not only instills trust in citizens, businesses, and investors, but also fosters a culture of responsible and ethical data management. Moreover, robust data privacy and security frameworks are essential for compliance with international standards and regulations, which in turn can facilitate cross-border data flows and contribute to the region's economic growth and development.

Key Concerns in the Middle East

1. *Fragmented and Inconsistent Legal Frameworks:* The Middle East faces the challenge of creating harmonized and comprehensive data protection regulations. The absence of a unified legal framework results in a patchwork of national laws that can vary widely in scope and implementation. This inconsistency creates confusion and uncertainty for businesses and individuals alike, making it difficult to ensure compliance and hindering the region's ability to establish a cohesive approach to data privacy and security.
2. *Cybersecurity Threats:* The Middle East is no stranger to cybersecurity threats, with several high-profile attacks in recent years highlighting the vulnerability of the region's digital infrastructure. The growing sophistication and prevalence of cyberattacks make the task of securing data and safeguarding privacy all the more urgent, necessitating a proactive and coordinated approach to cybersecurity.
3. *Cultural Factors:* The Middle East's diverse cultural landscape can present challenges when it comes to data privacy and security. In some instances, cultural norms and practices may conflict with modern data protection principles, necessitating a delicate balancing act to ensure that both cultural values and privacy rights are respected.
4. *Limited Awareness and Expertise:* The issue of data privacy and security is still relatively new in the Middle East, and as such, there is often a lack of awareness and understanding among both the public and private sectors. This knowledge gap can make it difficult for organizations to implement effective data protection measures, increasing the risk of breaches and violations.

Addressing Data Privacy and Security Concerns in the Middle East

To tackle the challenges of data privacy and security in the region, Middle Eastern countries must adopt a multifaceted approach that encompasses legal, technological, and educational measures.

1. Developing Comprehensive Legal Frameworks: Middle Eastern countries should prioritize the creation of comprehensive and harmonized data protection laws that adhere to international standards. By establishing clear and consistent regulations, the region can promote trust and transparency, fostering a more secure and privacy-focused data governance ecosystem.
2. Strengthening Cybersecurity Infrastructure: Investing in robust cybersecurity measures is essential for safeguarding data privacy and security. This includes the development of secure digital infrastructure, the implementation of advanced threat detection and response mechanisms, and the promotion of public-private partnerships to share expertise and resources.
3. Promoting a Culture of Privacy: Raising awareness about the importance of data privacy and security among citizens, businesses, and government entities is critical to fostering a culture that values and respects privacy rights. This can be achieved through public education campaigns, training programs for organizations, and the development of privacy-focused industry standards and best practices.
4. Building Expertise and Capacity: The Middle East must invest in developing the necessary human capital to support effective data privacy and security measures. This includes offering education and training programs in data protection, privacy law, and cybersecurity, as well as supporting research and development in these areas

The Middle East faces a unique set of challenges when it comes to data privacy and security. Addressing these concerns requires a concerted effort from governments, businesses, and individuals alike, as they work together to create a robust data protection ecosystem that safeguards privacy rights and promotes trust.

As the Middle East continues to embrace digital transformation and harness the power of data, it is vital that data privacy and security remain at the forefront of the region's data governance initiatives. Through this collaborative and multifaceted approach, the Middle East can not only address the pressing concerns of data privacy and security but also unlock new opportunities for innovation, economic growth, and societal advancement. By doing so, the region can demonstrate its commitment to responsible and ethical data management, reinforcing its position as a competitive player in the global digital landscape and paving the way for a more secure and prosperous future.

Cyber Threats and Vulnerabilities

The Middle East, a region characterized by rapid digital transformation and economic development, faces a growing array of cyber threats and vulnerabilities. These challenges not only pose a risk to data privacy and security but also have significant implications for the broader data governance landscape in the region. By understanding and addressing these cyber threats and vulnerabilities, Middle Eastern countries can seize the opportunities that effective data governance presents and strengthen their position in the global digital ecosystem.

Key Cyber Threats and Vulnerabilities in the Middle East

1. *State-Sponsored Cyber Attacks:* State-sponsored cyber-attacks are a significant concern in the Middle East, with various nation-states leveraging cyber espionage and sabotage to advance their geopolitical objectives. These attacks can target critical infrastructure, government

systems, and private sector organizations, potentially resulting in data breaches, service disruptions, and the theft of sensitive information.

2. *Cybercrime:* The Middle East has seen a surge in cybercrime in recent years, driven by factors such as the increased digitization of services, a growing reliance on digital payment systems, and the widespread use of social media platforms. Cybercriminals exploit these vulnerabilities to engage in activities such as identity theft, financial fraud, and data breaches, posing a considerable risk to data privacy and security.

3. *Insider Threats:* Insider threats are another critical vulnerability in the Middle Eastern data governance landscape. Disgruntled employees, contractors, or other insiders with access to sensitive information may intentionally or inadvertently compromise data security, resulting in breaches or leaks that can have severe consequences for organizations and individuals alike.

4. *Weak Cybersecurity Measures:* In many cases, organizations in the Middle East have not yet implemented robust cybersecurity measures that adequately protect against the growing array of threats. This can include inadequate encryption, outdated software, or a lack of security awareness among employees, all of which can leave systems and data vulnerable to cyberattacks.

Opportunities for Strengthening Data Governance in the Face of Cyber Threats and Vulnerabilities

1. *Collaborative Cybersecurity Efforts:* To effectively address the growing cyber threats and vulnerabilities in the region, Middle Eastern countries must collaborate and share information, resources, and expertise. This can include the establishment of regional cybersecurity centers, joint cyber defense exercises, and the development of shared threat intelligence platforms.

2. *Public-Private Partnerships:* Governments and private sector organizations in the Middle East should work together to strengthen data privacy and security. Public-private partnerships can facilitate the sharing of best practices, the development of innovative cybersecurity solutions, and the pooling of resources and expertise to address common challenges.

3. *Capacity Building and Education:* Building a skilled workforce with expertise in cybersecurity, data privacy, and data governance is crucial for addressing cyber threats and vulnerabilities in the Middle East. This can be achieved through investments in education and training programs, as well as the development of specialized courses and certifications in these areas.

4. *Regulatory Frameworks and Compliance:* Middle Eastern countries should establish comprehensive regulatory frameworks that promote data privacy, security, and compliance. By adopting international standards and best practices, the region can create a more resilient data governance ecosystem that is better equipped to withstand cyber threats and vulnerabilities.

The Middle East faces a complex array of cyber threats and vulnerabilities that have significant implications for data privacy, security, and governance in the region. By adopting a proactive and collaborative approach, Middle Eastern countries can address these challenges and seize the opportunities that effective data governance presents. By doing so, the region can strengthen its position in the global digital landscape and foster a more secure, prosperous, and interconnected future.

Strategies for Mitigating Risks

As the Middle East grapples with the challenges and opportunities of data governance, it is crucial to develop and implement strategies to mitigate the risks associated with data privacy and security. By addressing these concerns, the region can create a more resilient data governance ecosystem that fosters trust, innovation, and economic growth. Below are several strategies that Middle Eastern countries can adopt to mitigate risks in data privacy and security:

1. *Comprehensive Data Protection Legislation:* Developing and implementing comprehensive data protection legislation in line with international standards, such as the General Data Protection Regulation (GDPR), can provide a strong foundation for mitigating risks associated with data privacy and security. Such legislation should address key principles, including data minimization, purpose limitation, and transparency, to ensure that personal data is collected, processed, and stored responsibly and securely.
2. *Encourage Adoption of Privacy-by-Design Principles:* Encouraging businesses and organizations to adopt privacy-by-design principles can help to embed data privacy and security into the very fabric of their operations. This proactive approach ensures that privacy concerns are addressed from the outset of any project or initiative, reducing the likelihood of data breaches or privacy violations.
3. *Establishing a Robust Cybersecurity Framework:* Developing a robust cybersecurity framework that encompasses threat detection, prevention, and response is essential for protecting sensitive data from cyber threats. This should include regular risk assessments, the implementation of advanced security technologies, and the development of incident response plans to minimize the impact of security breaches.
4. *Strengthening International Cooperation:* Collaborating with international partners and organizations can help Middle Eastern countries share best practices, resources, and expertise in data privacy and security. This cooperation can lead to the development of joint initiatives, the exchange of threat intelligence, and the harmonization

of legal frameworks to create a more unified and resilient approach to data governance.

5. *Raising Public Awareness and Education:* Promoting awareness of data privacy and security issues among the general public and businesses is essential for fostering a culture of responsibility and compliance. This can be achieved through public education campaigns, workshops, and training programs that focus on the importance of data protection, the potential risks of data breaches, and the steps that individuals and organizations can take to protect their data.

6. *Developing Industry-Specific Guidelines and Best Practices:* Collaborating with industry stakeholders to develop sector-specific guidelines and best practices for data privacy and security can help to ensure that these issues are addressed in a tailored and context-specific manner. This can include the creation of industry standards, certifications, and codes of conduct that promote responsible data management practices.

7. *Investing in Human Capital:* Building a skilled workforce with expertise in data privacy, security, and governance is crucial for addressing the challenges and seizing the opportunities presented by data governance in the Middle East. This can be achieved through investments in education and training programs, as well as partnerships with academic institutions and industry experts.

Mitigating risks in data privacy and security concerns is a critical aspect of addressing the challenges and opportunities of data governance in the Middle East. By adopting a multifaceted approach that encompasses legal, technological, and educational measures, the region can build a resilient and secure data governance ecosystem that promotes trust, innovation, and economic growth.

Chapter 8

Ensuring Data Quality and Promoting Literacy

Addressing Data Quality and Integrity Issues

Ensuring data quality and integrity is of paramount importance in the age of digital transformation. High-quality, accurate, and reliable data is essential for organizations to make informed decisions, drive innovation, and maintain a competitive edge in today's data-driven landscape. Middle Eastern countries, like the rest of the world, must address data quality and integrity issues to effectively harness the power of data and build a strong data governance foundation. The following strategies can help address these challenges:

1. *Establish Data Governance Policies and Procedures:* Implementing clear and comprehensive data governance policies and procedures can provide a solid foundation for ensuring data quality and integrity. These policies should outline the roles and responsibilities of stakeholders, data management processes, and quality standards, ensuring that data is collected, processed, and maintained in a consistent and reliable manner.

2. *Data Quality Assurance Framework:* Developing a data quality assurance framework can help organizations systematically assess and improve the quality of their data. This framework should include key quality dimensions, such as accuracy, completeness, consistency,

timeliness, and relevance, and should be regularly reviewed and updated to reflect evolving data needs and priorities.

3. *Implement Data Validation and Verification Processes:* Establishing data validation and verification processes can help to ensure that data is accurate, consistent, and reliable. This can include automated validation checks, manual data review, and cross-referencing with external data sources to identify and correct errors and discrepancies.

4. *Data Stewardship:* Appointing data stewards within organizations can help to ensure that data quality and integrity are maintained throughout the data lifecycle. Data stewards are responsible for overseeing data management processes, addressing data quality issues, and ensuring that data adheres to organizational standards and policies.

5. *Encourage a Data Quality Culture:* Fostering a culture that values data quality and integrity is essential for driving organizational commitment to data management best practices. This can be achieved through regular training and education programs, performance metrics that incorporate data quality, and leadership support for data governance initiatives.

6. *Utilize Data Quality Tools and Technologies:* Leveraging advanced data quality tools and technologies can help organizations automate and streamline their data management processes, reducing the risk of human error and improving overall data quality. This can include tools for data cleansing, deduplication, and profiling, as well as machine learning and artificial intelligence-based solutions for anomaly detection and data validation.

7. *Monitor and Measure Data Quality:* Establishing ongoing monitoring and measurement processes can help organizations track and assess data quality over time, enabling them to identify trends, patterns, and areas for improvement. This can include the development of data quality dashboards, key performance indicators (KPIs), and regular

data quality audits to ensure that data remains accurate, consistent, and reliable.

Addressing data quality and integrity issues is essential for organizations and countries seeking to harness the full potential of data in today's digital landscape. By implementing robust data governance policies, fostering a culture of data quality, and leveraging advanced tools and technologies, Middle Eastern countries can enhance their data management capabilities, driving innovation, and economic growth in the region.

Data management and storage solutions
data management and storage solutions play a crucial role in ensuring that data remains accurate, consistent, and secure throughout its lifecycle. The following data management and storage solutions can help organizations maintain high-quality data:

1. *Data Warehousing:* A data warehouse is a central repository for collecting, storing, and managing large volumes of structured and semi-structured data from various sources. Data warehouses provide a single source of truth, facilitating data integration, consolidation, and consistency, thereby improving data quality and integrity.
2. *Data Integration Tools:* Data integration tools help organizations collect and consolidate data from disparate sources, ensuring that the data is consistent, accurate, and up-to-date. These tools can include Extract, Transform, Load (ETL) processes, data mapping, and data blending solutions that enable organizations to merge and transform data from different systems into a unified view.
3. *Data Quality Management Software:* Data quality management software can help organizations identify, monitor, and resolve data quality issues through data profiling, cleansing, deduplication, and validation processes. By automating these tasks, organizations can

maintain high-quality data, reduce errors, and improve overall data integrity.

4. *Master Data Management (MDM):* MDM is a comprehensive approach to managing an organization's critical data, ensuring that a single, consistent, and accurate version of the data is maintained across multiple systems and applications. MDM helps organizations streamline their data management processes, reduce data duplication, and improve data quality and consistency.

5. *Data Backup and Recovery Solutions:* Ensuring that data is regularly backed up and can be easily recovered in the event of data loss or corruption is essential for maintaining data quality and integrity. Data backup and recovery solutions include cloud-based storage, offsite storage, and automated backup systems that safeguard data from potential risks, such as hardware failures, natural disasters, and cyberattacks.

6. *Data Encryption and Security Solutions:* Protecting data from unauthorized access, tampering, or theft is crucial for maintaining data quality and integrity. Data encryption and security solutions can include encryption protocols, access controls, and secure storage systems that safeguard sensitive data from both internal and external threats.

7. *Data Lifecycle Management (DLM):* DLM is an approach to managing data from its creation to its eventual retirement, ensuring that data quality and integrity are maintained throughout its lifecycle. DLM processes can include data archiving, data retention policies, and data disposal procedures that help organizations manage their data more effectively and securely.

Data management and storage solutions are essential tools for addressing data quality and integrity issues. By implementing these solutions, organizations can ensure that their data remains accurate, consistent, and secure, providing a reliable foundation for decision-making and innovation. As Middle Eastern countries continue to embrace digital transformation and harness the power of data, adopting robust data management and storage solutions will be crucial for maintaining data quality and integrity across the region.

Implementing data quality frameworks

Implementing data quality frameworks in the Middle East can significantly contribute to addressing data quality and integrity issues. These frameworks provide a structured approach for organizations to assess, monitor, and improve their data management processes, ensuring that data remains accurate, consistent, and reliable. The following steps outline how to implement data quality frameworks in the Middle East:

1. *Define Data Quality Dimensions:* Establish a clear set of data quality dimensions that reflect the specific needs and priorities of organizations in the Middle East. Common dimensions include accuracy, completeness, consistency, timeliness, and relevance. These dimensions provide a basis for assessing and measuring data quality, as well as identifying areas for improvement.
2. *Develop Data Quality Metrics and Indicators:* Create a set of metrics and indicators that can be used to measure data quality across the defined dimensions. These metrics should be quantifiable, objective, and relevant to the specific data management processes and systems in use within the organization.
3. *Establish Data Quality Policies and Procedures:* Develop and implement data quality policies and procedures that outline the roles, responsibilities, and processes for maintaining and improving data quality. These policies should provide clear guidance on data collection, storage, processing, and validation, ensuring that data is managed consistently and effectively across the organization.

4. *Allocate Resources and Establish Ownership:* Assign dedicated resources and establish clear ownership for data quality initiatives within the organization. This can include appointing data stewards or data quality teams who are responsible for overseeing data management processes, addressing data quality issues, and ensuring that data adheres to organizational standards and policies.

5. *Implement Data Quality Tools and Technologies:* Leverage advanced data quality tools and technologies to automate and streamline data management processes. This can include tools for data cleansing, deduplication, profiling, and validation, as well as machine learning and artificial intelligence-based solutions for anomaly detection and data enrichment.

6. *Continuous Monitoring and Improvement:* Establish ongoing monitoring and improvement processes to track and assess data quality over time. This can include regular data quality audits, the development of data quality dashboards, and the use of key performance indicators (KPIs) to measure progress against established data quality objectives.

7. *Training and Education:* Provide regular training and education programs for employees to promote awareness of data quality issues and best practices. Encouraging a culture of data quality within the organization is essential for driving commitment to data management processes and ensuring the success of data quality initiatives.

8. *Collaboration and Knowledge Sharing:* Encourage collaboration and knowledge sharing among organizations, industry stakeholders, and government entities in the Middle East to exchange best practices, lessons learned, and innovative solutions for addressing data quality and integrity issues.

By implementing these data quality frameworks in the Middle East, organizations can establish a strong foundation for data governance, ensuring that their data remains accurate, consistent, and reliable. This, in turn, can help drive informed decision-making, foster innovation, and support economic growth across the region.

Promoting data literacy and skills development

As the digital transformation accelerates globally, promoting data literacy and skills development is essential for harnessing the full potential of data in the Middle East. Data literacy is the ability to read, analyze, interpret, and communicate data effectively, while skills development encompasses the broader set of technical and analytical capabilities required for working with data. The following strategies can help promote data literacy and skills development in the Middle East:

1. *Integrate Data Literacy into Educational Curricula:* Incorporating data literacy into primary, secondary, and tertiary educational curricula can ensure that students develop the necessary skills from an early age. This can include integrating data analysis, visualization, and interpretation exercises into subjects such as mathematics, science, and social studies.

2. *Develop Specialized Data Science and Analytics Programs:* Establishing dedicated data science and analytics programs at universities and vocational institutions can help produce a skilled workforce capable of addressing the region's growing data needs. These programs should cover key topics such as statistics, machine learning, data visualization, and programming languages like Python and R.

3. *Collaborate with Industry and Government:* Fostering partnerships between educational institutions, industry stakeholders, and government entities can help align skills development initiatives with the specific needs of the region's job market. These collaborations can result in the creation of industry-driven curricula, internships, and joint

research projects that bridge the gap between academia and the professional world.

4. *Leverage Online Learning Platforms:* Online learning platforms, such as Coursera, edX, and LinkedIn Learning, can provide accessible and affordable opportunities for individuals to develop their data skills. Encouraging the use of these platforms and offering financial incentives, such as scholarships or grants, can help make data literacy and skills development more accessible to a wider audience.

5. *Establish Data Literacy and Skills Development Initiatives:* Governments and organizations can develop targeted initiatives, such as training programs, workshops, and hackathons, to promote data literacy and skills development across various sectors. These initiatives can help raise awareness of the importance of data skills and provide practical, hands-on learning experiences for participants.

6. *Create Communities of Practice:* Encouraging the establishment of data-related communities of practice, such as meetups, user groups, and online forums, can provide opportunities for individuals to share knowledge, exchange ideas, and learn from one another. These communities can foster a sense of collaboration and support, helping to advance data literacy and skills development across the region.

7. *Incentivize Skills Development and Retention:* Offering incentives, such as tax breaks, professional development grants, or career advancement opportunities, can encourage individuals and organizations to invest in data literacy and skills development. These incentives can help retain skilled talent within the region and drive the growth of the local data ecosystem.

By promoting data literacy and skills development in the Middle East, the region can cultivate a skilled workforce capable of navigating the complex data landscape and driving innovation. In turn, this can help to unlock the full potential of data, fueling economic growth and strengthening the region's position as a global leader in the digital age.

Educational programs and training initiatives

Educational programs and training initiatives play a vital role in promoting data literacy and skills development. By providing individuals with the knowledge, skills, and competencies needed to work effectively with data, these programs can empower individuals to make informed decisions, drive innovation, and contribute to the growth of the data-driven economy. Here are several ways educational programs and training initiatives can contribute to promoting data literacy and skills development:

1. *Building a Strong Foundation:* Educational programs, starting from primary and secondary levels, can help students develop a strong foundation in data literacy by incorporating data-related concepts and activities into various subjects. This early exposure to data analysis, interpretation, and visualization can help students become more comfortable working with data and develop critical thinking skills that will serve them well in their future careers.

2. *Developing Technical Skills:* Specialized educational programs, such as data science or analytics degrees, can equip students with the technical skills needed to work effectively with data. These programs often cover essential topics, including programming languages, statistics, machine learning, and data visualization, preparing students to tackle complex data challenges in the professional world.

3. *Enhancing Soft Skills:* In addition to technical skills, educational programs and training initiatives can also help develop essential soft skills, such as communication, teamwork, and problem-solving. These skills are crucial for working with data, as they enable individuals to effectively communicate insights, collaborate with diverse teams, and approach data-driven problems creatively.

4. *Providing Hands-on Experience:* Training initiatives, such as workshops, hackathons, and internships, offer valuable hands-on experience, allowing individuals to apply their data skills to real-world situations. This practical experience can help participants gain a

deeper understanding of the challenges and opportunities in working with data and build their confidence in using data to make informed decisions.

5. *Expanding Access to Education:* Online learning platforms and training initiatives can make data literacy and skills development more accessible to a wider audience. By offering flexible, affordable, and scalable learning opportunities, these platforms can help break down barriers to education and empower individuals from diverse backgrounds to develop their data skills.

6. *Fostering a Data-Driven Culture:* Educational programs and training initiatives can help promote a data-driven culture within organizations and communities. By raising awareness of the importance of data literacy and skills development, these programs can encourage individuals to embrace data-driven decision-making and view data as a valuable asset.

7. *Creating Networking Opportunities:* Educational programs and training initiatives can provide valuable networking opportunities for participants, connecting them with industry professionals, academics, and peers who share similar interests. These connections can lead to new career opportunities, collaborations, and ongoing learning experiences that contribute to personal and professional growth.

Educational programs and training initiatives are essential tools for promoting data literacy and skills development. By providing individuals with the knowledge, skills, and experiences needed to work effectively with data, these programs can empower individuals to drive innovation, make informed decisions, and contribute to the growth of the data-driven economy.

The role of universities and research institutions

Universities and research institutions play a critical role in promoting data literacy and skills development. As centers of knowledge and innovation, they are well-positioned to create and disseminate data-related knowledge, foster collaboration, and cultivate a skilled workforce capable of addressing the challenges and opportunities presented by the data-driven economy. The following are some ways in which universities and research institutions contribute to promoting data literacy and skills development:

1. *Offering Specialized Degree Programs:* Universities can develop and offer specialized degree programs in data science, analytics, and related fields to train students in the technical and analytical skills required to work with data effectively. These programs can cover essential topics such as statistics, machine learning, data visualization, and programming languages, preparing students for careers in the data-driven economy.

2. *Integrating Data Literacy into Existing Curricula:* Universities and research institutions can integrate data literacy concepts and activities into existing curricula across various disciplines, including social sciences, humanities, and engineering. This interdisciplinary approach to data literacy ensures that students from diverse backgrounds develop the skills needed to work effectively with data in their respective fields.

3. *Conducting Cutting-Edge Research:* Research institutions can advance the field of data science and analytics by conducting innovative research projects, exploring new methodologies, and developing novel applications of data. This research can help identify emerging trends, address pressing challenges, and drive the development of new tools and techniques that enhance data literacy and skills development.

4. *Providing Training and Professional Development Opportunities:* Universities and research institutions can offer workshops, seminars,

and short courses to professionals seeking to develop their data literacy and skills. These opportunities can help individuals stay current with the latest trends and best practices in data management and analysis, ensuring they remain competitive in the job market.

5. *Fostering Collaboration and Knowledge Exchange:* Universities and research institutions can serve as hubs for collaboration and knowledge exchange, connecting students, researchers, industry professionals, and policymakers interested in data-related topics. These connections can lead to the development of new research projects, partnerships, and educational initiatives that further promote data literacy and skills development.

6. *Creating Data-Driven Learning Environments:* Universities and research institutions can leverage data and analytics to enhance teaching and learning experiences. By incorporating data-driven tools and techniques into the classroom, educators can provide students with hands-on experience in working with data and foster a culture of data-driven decision-making.

7. *Engaging with Industry and Government:* Universities and research institutions can collaborate with industry and government stakeholders to align their educational and research efforts with the needs of the job market and public policy objectives. These collaborations can result in the development of industry-driven curricula, internships, and joint research projects that bridge the gap between academia and practice.

Universities and research institutions play a crucial role in promoting data literacy and skills development. Through their educational programs, research initiatives, and collaborative efforts, these institutions can cultivate a skilled workforce, drive innovation, and contribute to the growth of the data-driven economy.

Chapter 9

Middle Eastern Success Stories

Smart cities and data-driven urban planning

In recent years, smart cities and data-driven urban planning projects have gained momentum in the Middle East, with governments and private sector organizations increasingly leveraging data and advanced technologies to improve the quality of life for citizens. Effective data governance plays a critical role in the success of these initiatives by ensuring data quality, privacy, and security. In this analysis, we will investigate examples of successful data governance implementations in smart cities and data-driven urban planning projects within the Middle East and discuss the potential lessons learned for other cities and regions.

Dubai Smart City Initiative

Dubai's Smart City Initiative is an ambitious program that aims to transform the city into one of the world's most advanced smart cities. The initiative focuses on six key dimensions: smart life, smart economy, smart governance, smart environment, smart mobility, and smart people. Data governance plays a crucial role in this initiative, with the Dubai Data Establishment (DDE) responsible for overseeing the city's data strategy, policies, and standards. Effective data governance practices have been instrumental in the success of Dubai's Smart City Initiative, enabling the integration and sharing of data across various government entities and private sector organizations. Some notable achievements of the initiative include the launch of the Dubai Pulse platform, which provides access to city-wide data sets, and the implementation of the Dubai Data Law, which sets guidelines for data classification, sharing, and protection.

Effective data governance is essential for the success of smart city initiatives, as it ensures data quality, security, and privacy while fostering data sharing and collaboration among various stakeholders.

Masdar City, Abu Dhabi

Masdar City, a planned city in Abu Dhabi, is designed to be a sustainable, carbon-neutral urban development driven by renewable energy sources and advanced technologies. Data governance is a crucial component of Masdar City's development, as the city relies on accurate and timely data to optimize energy consumption, monitor environmental conditions, and improve urban planning decisions. Masdar City has established a robust data governance framework that includes data privacy and security policies, data quality management processes, and data sharing agreements with various stakeholders. These data governance practices have contributed to the city's success in achieving its sustainability goals and creating a data-driven urban environment.

Robust data governance practices can enable cities to harness data effectively for sustainable and data-driven urban planning, ensuring that the benefits of smart city initiatives are realized while protecting the privacy and security of citizen data.

Riyadh Smart City, Saudi Arabia

Riyadh, the capital city of Saudi Arabia, has embarked on a journey to become a smart city as part of the country's Vision 2030 plan. The Riyadh Smart City initiative focuses on improving the quality of life for residents by leveraging data and advanced technologies in areas such as transportation, healthcare, education, and public safety. The success of Riyadh's Smart City initiative can be attributed to its effective data governance practices, which include the development of data sharing platforms, the establishment of data privacy and security policies, and the implementation of data quality management processes. These data governance practices have enabled the city to harness the power of data to improve urban planning and service delivery, while also ensuring the protection of citizen data.

Effective data governance practices can help cities overcome the challenges associated with managing large volumes of data from various sources and ensure that data-driven urban planning initiatives are successful and sustainable.

Madinah Smart City, Saudi Arabia

Madinah, the second holiest city in Islam, has launched a smart city initiative to improve the quality of life for its residents and visitors while preserving its religious and historical significance. The initiative focuses on several key areas, such as smart infrastructure, transportation, public safety, and environmental sustainability. Effective data governance has played a critical role in Madinah's smart city transformation, with the city implementing data management policies, data sharing agreements, and data quality processes to ensure the accuracy, security, and privacy of data. The city has also developed the Madinah Integrated Command & Control

Center (MICCC), which gathers data from various sources to monitor and manage city-wide operations.

Successful smart city initiatives require a strong data governance foundation that balances innovation with the preservation of cultural and historical values, ensuring that the benefits of digital transformation are realized without compromising the unique identity of the city.

Neom, Saudi Arabia

Neom, a futuristic mega-city project in Saudi Arabia, aims to create a new model for sustainable living by leveraging advanced technologies and data-driven solutions. The city's development focuses on several key areas, such as energy, water, transportation, and biotechnology. Data governance plays a central role in Neom's vision, with the project emphasizing the importance of data quality, privacy, and security to create a truly connected and sustainable urban environment. Neom has adopted international best practices in data governance, such as GDPR, to ensure that data is managed effectively and responsibly.

Integrating data governance principles from the early stages of a mega-city project ensures that data-driven solutions are implemented responsibly, helping to create a sustainable and connected urban environment.

Tel Aviv, Israel

Tel Aviv, a vibrant and tech-savvy city in Israel, has implemented a range of smart city initiatives aimed at improving the quality of life for its residents. The city focuses on areas such as transportation, public safety, and environmental sustainability, leveraging data and technology to drive innovation and improve urban planning decisions. Data governance has played a crucial role in Tel Aviv's smart city initiatives, with the city adopting a comprehensive data governance framework that includes data privacy and security policies, data quality management processes, and data sharing agreements with stakeholders. Tel Aviv's DigiTel Residents Club, a data-driven platform that provides personalized city services, is an example of how effective data governance can contribute to the success of smart city initiatives.

Embracing data governance best practices helps cities harness the power of data to drive innovation and improve the quality of life for their residents, while also ensuring that privacy and security concerns are addressed.

Healthcare data management and patient privacy
Cleveland Clinic Abu Dhabi, United Arab Emirates

Cleveland Clinic Abu Dhabi, a leading healthcare provider in the UAE, has implemented robust data governance practices to manage patient data, ensuring privacy, security, and regulatory compliance. The hospital has adopted an electronic medical records (EMR) system that adheres to international standards, such as HIPAA, as well as local regulations. Effective data governance has contributed to the hospital's ability to deliver high-quality healthcare by enabling seamless data sharing among healthcare professionals while maintaining patient privacy. The hospital's data-driven approach has also led to improved patient outcomes and more personalized care.

King Faisal Specialist Hospital and Research Centre, Saudi Arabia

King Faisal Specialist Hospital and Research Centre in Saudi Arabia has adopted a comprehensive data governance framework to manage its vast collection of patient data, research, and clinical trials. The framework includes data classification, access control, and data quality management processes to ensure data accuracy and security. As a result of effective data governance, the hospital has been able to provide cutting-edge healthcare services and contribute to medical research advancements. The data-driven approach has led to more accurate diagnoses and personalized treatments, ultimately improving patient outcomes.

Dubai Health Authority (DHA), United Arab Emirates

The Dubai Health Authority (DHA) has implemented the Salama Electronic Medical Record (EMR) system across all its healthcare facilities, including hospitals and primary healthcare centers. This initiative is built upon strong data governance practices, ensuring data privacy, security, and compliance with local and international regulations. Effective data governance has allowed DHA facilities to provide better care coordination and patient management. The centralized system ensures that healthcare providers have access to accurate and up-to-date patient information, leading to improved patient outcomes and increased efficiency in the healthcare sector.

Hamad Medical Corporation (HMC), Qatar

Hamad Medical Corporation (HMC) in Qatar has adopted a robust data governance framework to manage its electronic health records (EHR) system across multiple healthcare facilities. This framework includes data quality management, privacy, and security policies to ensure compliance with local and international regulations. The successful implementation of data governance practices has enabled HMC to deliver high-quality healthcare services, reduce medical errors, and improve patient outcomes. The data-driven approach has also allowed for better decision-making and resource allocation, contributing to the overall efficiency of the healthcare system.

Sheba Medical Center, Israel

Sheba Medical Center in Israel has embraced data governance practices to manage its extensive patient data and support its cutting-edge research initiatives. The center has implemented strict data privacy and security policies, as well as data quality management processes to ensure compliance with local and international regulations. Effective data governance at Sheba Medical Center has facilitated improved patient care by enabling healthcare professionals to make data-driven decisions, leading to more accurate diagnoses and personalized treatments. Additionally, the center's commitment to data governance has supported its research efforts, driving innovation and contributing to the advancement of medical knowledge.

Johns Hopkins Aramco Healthcare (JHAH), Saudi Arabia

Johns Hopkins Aramco Healthcare (JHAH) in Saudi Arabia has implemented a robust data governance framework to manage its patient data and ensure compliance with local and international regulations. The organization has adopted an advanced electronic health records (EHR) system that prioritizes data privacy, security, and quality. Effective data governance has allowed JHAH to deliver high-quality healthcare services, leading to improved patient outcomes and satisfaction. The organization's data-driven approach has also facilitated more efficient resource allocation and better decision-making, contributing to overall healthcare system optimization.

Al Jalila Children's Specialty Hospital, United Arab Emirates

Al Jalila Children's Specialty Hospital in Dubai has focused on strong data governance practices in managing its electronic medical records (EMR) system. The hospital has implemented strict data privacy and security policies, as well as data quality management processes, to ensure compliance with local and international regulations. By adopting effective data governance practices, Al Jalila Children's Specialty Hospital has been able to provide improved patient care, resulting in better health outcomes for children. The data-driven approach has allowed for more accurate diagnoses, personalized treatments, and efficient coordination of care.

American University of Beirut Medical Center (AUBMC), Lebanon

The American University of Beirut Medical Center (AUBMC) has implemented a comprehensive data governance framework to manage patient data, research initiatives, and clinical trials. The framework includes data classification, access control, and data quality management processes to ensure data accuracy, privacy, and security. As a result of effective data governance, AUBMC has been able to deliver cutting-edge healthcare services, contribute to medical research advancements, and improve patient outcomes. The data-driven approach has also facilitated better decision-making and more efficient resource allocation within the healthcare system.

Sidra Medicine, Qatar

Sidra Medicine in Qatar has adopted a robust data governance framework to manage its electronic health records (EHR) system across its state-of-the-art facilities. This framework includes data quality management, privacy, and security policies to ensure compliance with local and international regulations. The successful implementation of data governance practices has enabled Sidra Medicine to deliver high-quality healthcare services, reduce medical errors, and improve patient outcomes. The data-driven approach has also allowed for better decision-making, resource allocation, and innovation within the healthcare system.

Hadassah Medical Center, Israel

Hadassah Medical Center in Israel has embraced data governance practices to manage its extensive patient data and support its research initiatives. The center has implemented strict data privacy and security policies, as well as data quality management processes to ensure compliance with local and international regulations. Effective data governance at Hadassah Medical Center has facilitated improved patient care by enabling healthcare professionals to make data-driven decisions, leading to more accurate diagnoses and personalized treatments. Additionally, the center's commitment to data governance has supported its research efforts, driving innovation and contributing to the advancement of medical knowledge.

These case studies demonstrate the significant impact of effective data governance practices on healthcare quality, patient outcomes, and regulatory compliance in the Middle East. By adopting robust data governance frameworks, healthcare providers can harness the power of data to drive improvements in patient care and contribute to the overall efficiency and innovation within the healthcare sector.

Financial sector compliance and data transparency
Emirates NBD, United Arab Emirates

Emirates NBD, a leading bank in the UAE, has successfully implemented a comprehensive data governance framework to ensure data quality, privacy, and security. This has enabled the bank to maintain regulatory compliance and achieve data transparency, fostering trust with customers and stakeholders. The effective data governance practices have contributed to better decision-making, risk management, and overall financial stability.

Qatar National Bank (QNB), Qatar

Qatar National Bank (QNB) has embraced data governance to manage its vast financial data and ensure compliance with local and international regulations. The bank's data governance framework includes data classification, access control, and data quality management processes. These efforts have led to improved data transparency, enhanced risk management, and increased operational efficiency.

National Commercial Bank (NCB), Saudi Arabia

National Commercial Bank (NCB) in Saudi Arabia has adopted a robust data governance framework to manage its financial data and maintain compliance with regulatory requirements. The bank has successfully achieved data transparency by implementing strict data quality management and privacy policies. As a result, NCB has been able to better manage risks, improve customer service, and maintain the overall stability of the financial system.

Central Bank of the United Arab Emirates

The Central Bank of the UAE has effectively implemented data governance practices to manage its financial data and ensure compliance with local and international regulations. The bank's data governance framework includes data classification, access control, and data quality management processes. These efforts have led to improved data transparency, enhanced risk management, and increased operational efficiency, promoting financial stability in the region.

Bank Muscat, Oman

Bank Muscat, the largest bank in Oman, has successfully implemented a comprehensive data governance framework to manage its financial data and ensure compliance with local and international regulations. The bank's data governance practices have contributed to better decision-making, risk management, and overall financial stability, creating a more secure and transparent banking environment.

Arab Bank, Jordan

Arab Bank in Jordan has embraced data governance to manage its financial data and maintain regulatory compliance. The bank has implemented a robust data governance framework, including data classification, access control, and data quality management processes. This has resulted in improved data transparency, enhanced risk management, and increased operational efficiency.

National Bank of Kuwait (NBK), Kuwait

National Bank of Kuwait (NBK) has successfully adopted a comprehensive data governance framework to manage its financial data and maintain compliance with regulatory requirements. The bank's data governance practices have contributed to better decision-making, risk management, and overall financial stability. The effective data governance efforts have fostered trust with customers and stakeholders and ensured the bank's continued success.

Bank Hapoalim, Israel

Bank Hapoalim in Israel has implemented a robust data governance framework to manage its financial data and ensure compliance with local and international regulations. The bank has successfully achieved data transparency by implementing strict data quality management and privacy policies. As a result, Bank Hapoalim has been able to better manage risks, improve customer service, and maintain the overall stability of the financial system.

Banque du Liban, Lebanon

The Central Bank of Lebanon, Banque du Liban, has embraced data governance practices to manage its financial data and ensure compliance with local and international regulations. The bank's data governance framework includes data classification, access control, and data quality management processes. These efforts have led to improved data transparency, enhanced risk management, and increased operational efficiency, promoting financial stability in the region.

Bahrain Islamic Bank, Bahrain

Bahrain Islamic Bank has adopted a comprehensive data governance framework to manage its financial data and maintain compliance with regulatory requirements. The bank's data governance practices have contributed to better decision-making, risk management, and overall financial stability. The effective data governance efforts have fostered trust with customers and stakeholders, ensuring the bank's continued success in the Islamic finance sector.

These case studies from the Middle Eastern financial sector demonstrate the significant benefits of implementing robust data governance practices. By achieving compliance and data transparency, financial institutions in the region have been able to improve decision-making, enhance risk management, and maintain overall financial stability. The success of these data governance efforts highlights the importance of data management and regulatory compliance in the financial sector, paving the way for a more secure and transparent financial environment in the Middle East. It also offers valuable insights and lessons for other financial institutions looking to strengthen their data governance practices and contribute to the overall stability of the financial system.

Cross-border data sharing for regional cooperation

As a data governance professional, it is important to examine the role of effective data governance in facilitating regional cooperation and development in the Middle East. Cross-border data sharing initiatives have become increasingly vital to the region, particularly in areas such as security, trade, and public health. In this analysis, we will investigate several successful cross-border data sharing initiatives that have contributed to regional cooperation, focusing on the role of data governance in ensuring the security and privacy of shared data and the broader implications for regional collaboration and development.

- *The Gulf Cooperation Council (GCC) Interconnection Grid:* The GCC Interconnection Grid is an ambitious project that aims to connect the electricity networks of six Gulf countries: Saudi Arabia, United Arab Emirates, Qatar, Kuwait, Bahrain, and Oman. The project relies on effective data governance and the secure exchange of information to ensure the stability and reliability of the interconnected grid. Data governance practices in this initiative involve establishing strict protocols for data security, privacy, and transmission, thereby fostering trust among the participating countries and ensuring the smooth functioning of the interconnected grid. The success of this initiative has had a significant positive impact on regional energy security and has facilitated the efficient sharing of electricity resources among GCC countries.

- *The Middle East and North Africa (MENA) Health Policy Forum:* The MENA Health Policy Forum is a regional platform that facilitates the exchange of healthcare data and best practices among countries in the region. This initiative is particularly important for public health surveillance, early warning systems, and addressing cross-border health threats, such as infectious diseases. Effective data governance is essential in ensuring the privacy and security of sensitive health data, as well as enabling the timely exchange of critical information between countries. The successful implementation of data governance practices in this initiative has led to improved regional collaboration on public health issues and has enhanced the overall health security of the MENA region.

- *The Arab Common Market for Information Technology (ACMIT):* The ACMIT is a regional initiative that aims to promote the development and integration of the ICT sector in the Arab world. One of the key objectives of this initiative is to facilitate the secure exchange of data and information among participating countries. Effective data governance practices are crucial in ensuring data privacy, security, and compliance with relevant regulations. The success of this initiative has led to increased regional cooperation in the ICT sector, fostering innovation and contributing to economic development in the Middle East.

- *The Regional Drought Monitoring and Early Warning System:* This cross-border initiative, which involves several Middle Eastern countries, aims to establish a regional drought monitoring and early warning system to mitigate the impacts of climate change on water resources. The secure and timely exchange of data, such as satellite imagery and meteorological information, is vital to the success of this initiative. Effective data governance practices ensure data accuracy, privacy, and security, enabling participating countries to share critical information with confidence. The success of this initiative has enhanced regional cooperation in addressing climate change and water resource management challenges.

- *The Middle East and North Africa Financial Action Task Force (MENAFATF):* The MENAFATF is a regional organization that focuses on combating money laundering and terrorist financing. The secure exchange of financial intelligence and data among participating countries is a critical aspect of this initiative. Effective data governance practices ensure the privacy and security of sensitive financial data while facilitating cooperation and information sharing among countries. The success of this initiative has led to a more robust regional effort to combat financial crimes and promote stability in the financial sector.

- *The Middle East and North Africa Cybersecurity Coalition (MENACC):* The MENACC is a regional initiative that aims to enhance cybersecurity cooperation among countries in the Middle East and North Africa. By sharing cybersecurity threat intelligence, best practices, and technical resources, participating countries can better defend against cyber threats and enhance their overall cybersecurity posture. Effective data governance is critical in ensuring the secure and timely exchange of sensitive cybersecurity information. The success of this initiative has strengthened regional collaboration on cybersecurity issues, ultimately leading to a more secure and resilient digital environment in the region.

- *The Arab Satellite Communications Organization (ARABSAT):* ARABSAT is a regional satellite communications organization that provides satellite services to countries across the Arab world. Secure data sharing and collaboration are essential for the effective functioning of satellite communications systems. Effective data governance practices ensure the security, privacy, and accuracy of shared satellite data, fostering trust among participating countries and facilitating the efficient exchange of information. The success of this initiative has led to improved regional satellite communication services, supporting economic growth and development in the Middle East.

- *The Regional Center for Renewable Energy and Energy Efficiency (RCREEE):* The RCREEE is a regional organization that promotes the adoption of renewable energy and energy efficiency practices in the Middle East and North Africa. The center facilitates the exchange of data, best practices, and technical resources among participating countries, enabling them to make informed decisions about renewable energy projects and energy efficiency measures. Effective data governance practices are crucial for ensuring the privacy, security, and accuracy of shared data, which in turn fosters trust and collaboration among countries in the region. The success of this initiative has contributed to the growth of renewable energy and energy efficiency in the Middle East, ultimately supporting regional sustainability and environmental goals.

- *The Middle East and North Africa Transport and Logistics Data Exchange (MENATLDX):* The MENATLDX is a regional initiative that aims to enhance the efficiency and competitiveness of the transportation and logistics sector in the Middle East and North Africa. By sharing data on freight movements, transportation infrastructure, and logistics services, participating countries can identify bottlenecks, optimize transportation routes, and improve overall supply chain efficiency. Effective data governance practices are essential for ensuring the privacy, security, and accuracy of shared data, which in turn fosters trust and collaboration among countries in the region. The success of this initiative has led to increased regional cooperation in the transport and logistics sector, promoting economic growth and development in the Middle East.

- *The Middle East and North Africa Environmental Data Exchange (MENAEDX):* The MENAEDX is a regional initiative that facilitates the exchange of environmental data among countries in the Middle East and North Africa. This initiative supports efforts to monitor and address environmental challenges, such as air and water pollution, biodiversity loss, and climate change. Effective data governance practices are critical for ensuring the privacy, security, and accuracy of shared environmental data, fostering trust and collaboration among participating countries. The success of this initiative has led to enhanced regional cooperation on environmental issues, ultimately supporting the sustainable development and environmental conservation goals of the Middle East.

These examples of successful cross-border data sharing initiatives in the Middle East demonstrate the importance of effective data governance in facilitating regional cooperation and development. By ensuring the security, privacy, and accuracy of shared data, data governance practices contribute to building trust and fostering collaboration among countries in the region. These initiatives also highlight the potential for data governance to play a crucial role in addressing some of the most pressing challenges facing the Middle East, such as climate change, public health, financial stability, and energy security.

Part IV

Looking Forward

Chapter 10

Innovations and Evolutions in Data Governance

The Future of Data Governance in the Middle East

The future of data governance in the Middle East is complex and multi-faceted, shaped by a diverse array of factors, including technological advancements, evolving regional dynamics, and global trends in data protection and privacy. As a data governance scholar, several critical aspects need to be considered when analyzing the future of data governance in the region.

1. *Technological advancements:* The rapid pace of technological development, including the growth of big data, artificial intelligence, the Internet of Things (IoT), and blockchain, has significant implications for data governance in the Middle East. These technologies generate vast amounts of data, requiring robust governance frameworks to ensure data privacy, security, and compliance. The ability of Middle Eastern countries to adapt their data governance practices to accommodate these emerging technologies will be crucial for their digital transformation and economic competitiveness.

2. *Evolving regional dynamics:* The Middle East is a region characterized by diverse political, economic, and cultural landscapes, which influence data governance practices. As regional dynamics evolve,

countries in the Middle East will need to assess and adapt their data governance frameworks to address emerging challenges and opportunities. This may include increased regional cooperation and harmonization of data protection laws, promoting cross-border data flows, and enhancing data sovereignty.

3. *Global trends in data protection and privacy:* The Middle East's data governance landscape will be influenced by global trends in data protection and privacy, such as the European Union's General Data Protection Regulation (GDPR) and the California Consumer Privacy Act (CCPA). These regulatory frameworks set new benchmarks for data protection and privacy, and Middle Eastern countries will need to adapt their data governance practices to align with these global standards.

4. *Public awareness and demand for data protection:* As public awareness of data privacy and security issues grows, there will likely be increased demand for stronger data protection measures in the Middle East. This could lead to the development of more comprehensive data protection laws and the establishment of dedicated data protection authorities to oversee data governance practices.

5. *Private sector innovation and collaboration:* The private sector will play a crucial role in shaping the future of data governance in the Middle East. As businesses increasingly recognize the value of data and the importance of effective data governance, they will need to adopt best practices, invest in cutting-edge technologies, and collaborate with public sector institutions to develop robust and innovative data governance frameworks.

6. *Capacity building and education:* The future of data governance in the Middle East will depend on the development of human capital and the cultivation of data governance expertise. This will require investment

in education and training programs, as well as the establishment of centers of excellence for data governance research and practice.

7. *Ethical considerations:* As data governance practices evolve, ethical considerations related to data usage, transparency, and consent will become increasingly important. Middle Eastern countries will need to develop ethical guidelines and frameworks to ensure that data governance practices respect individual rights and promote the public good.

The future of data governance in the Middle East is shaped by a multitude of factors, from technological advancements and evolving regional dynamics to global trends in data protection and privacy. By considering these factors and adapting data governance practices accordingly, the Middle East can unlock the full potential of data-driven innovation, enhance digital transformation, and foster economic growth and development.

Emerging technologies and their implications

Artificial intelligence and machine learning

The rapid development and adoption of artificial intelligence (AI) and machine learning (ML) technologies are reshaping various aspects of society, and data governance practices are no exception. In the Middle East, the impact of AI and ML on data governance will be multifaceted, influencing data management, data privacy, and data security. This analysis will examine the potential implications of AI and ML for data governance practices in the Middle East, focusing on the challenges and opportunities these technologies present.

Data Management

AI and ML technologies have the potential to significantly enhance data management processes in the Middle East. By automating routine tasks and leveraging advanced analytics, organizations can streamline data collection, storage, and processing, improving efficiency and reducing human error. For example, AI-powered data cataloging tools can automatically discover, classify, and annotate data, making it easier for organizations to maintain accurate and up-to-date records. Additionally, ML algorithms can be used to identify and correct data quality issues, ensuring that organizations have access to reliable and trustworthy information. However, the widespread adoption of AI and ML technologies also raises new data management challenges. The sheer volume of data generated by these technologies can strain existing data storage and processing infrastructure, requiring organizations to invest in scalable and flexible solutions, such as cloud-based platforms. Furthermore, the complexity of AI and ML models can make it difficult to trace data lineage and provenance, potentially leading to issues with data integrity and transparency.

Data Privacy

AI and ML technologies can both enhance and threaten data privacy in the Middle East. On the one hand, AI-powered tools can be used to automate privacy compliance tasks, such as identifying sensitive data, anonymizing records, and monitoring data access. For example, ML algorithms can automatically detect personally identifiable information (PII) within datasets and apply privacy-preserving techniques, such as data masking or differential privacy, to protect individuals' privacy. On the other hand, AI and ML technologies can also be used to infer sensitive information about individuals, even when data has been anonymized or aggregated. Techniques such as de-anonymization, data linkage, and adversarial attacks can exploit the predictive power of AI models to reveal private information, posing significant risks to data privacy. To address these challenges, organizations in the Middle East will need to adopt robust privacy-by-design principles and implement strong access controls and data usage policies.

Data Security

AI and ML technologies can play a crucial role in enhancing data security in the Middle East. By incorporating these technologies into their security infrastructure, organizations can detect and respond to threats more effectively and efficiently. For instance, AI-driven security solutions can analyze vast amounts of data in real-time, identifying patterns and anomalies that may indicate potential security breaches. Machine learning algorithms can also be used to strengthen authentication methods, such as biometric systems or behavioral analytics, reducing the risk of unauthorized access to sensitive data. Despite their potential to improve data security, AI and ML technologies also introduce new vulnerabilities. As cybercriminals increasingly adopt AI-powered tools and techniques, the sophistication of cyberattacks will continue to grow, posing significant challenges for organizations in the Middle East. Adversarial attacks targeting AI and ML models can compromise their accuracy and reliability, undermining the effectiveness of AI-driven security solutions. To mitigate these risks, organizations must invest in advanced threat intelligence and adopt a proactive approach to securing their AI and ML systems.

AI and ML technologies have the potential to significantly impact data governance practices in the Middle East. While these technologies offer numerous benefits, such as improved efficiency in data management, enhanced data privacy compliance, and strengthened data security, they also introduce new challenges and risks that must be carefully managed.

As the Middle East embraces the AI and ML revolution, organizations and governments will need to develop comprehensive data governance frameworks that address these emerging challenges while harnessing the full potential of these transformative technologies. This will require ongoing collaboration between stakeholders, investment in cutting-edge solutions, and the de

Blockchain and decentralized data management

Blockchain and decentralized data management technologies have the potential to significantly impact data governance in the Middle East. By leveraging the inherent characteristics of these technologies, such as immutability, transparency, and decentralization, organizations and governments in the region can improve data privacy, security, and compliance. This exploration will analyze the opportunities and challenges that blockchain and decentralized data management present for data governance in the Middle East.

Data Privacy

Blockchain technology can enhance data privacy in the Middle East by enabling more secure and transparent data-sharing practices. With decentralized data storage, individual users have greater control over their personal information, granting and revoking access as needed. Additionally, encryption and cryptographic techniques used in blockchain ensure that data remains secure and confidential during transmission and storage.

However, there are challenges related to data privacy in the context of blockchain. For instance, since blockchain networks are typically designed to be transparent, anonymizing data can be more complex. To address these concerns, developers must implement privacy-enhancing solutions, such as zero-knowledge proofs, confidential transactions, or off-chain data storage, to protect sensitive information while maintaining the benefits of blockchain technology.

Data Security

Blockchain's decentralized and immutable nature can enhance data security in the Middle East. By distributing data across multiple nodes in a network, the risk of data loss or unauthorized access is reduced. The immutability of blockchain also ensures that data cannot be tampered with or altered, providing a high level of trust and integrity.

Nonetheless, blockchain technology is not immune to security challenges. Vulnerabilities in smart contracts or consensus algorithms can be exploited by malicious actors, potentially compromising the security of the entire network. Organizations adopting blockchain solutions must diligently evaluate and address these security concerns to ensure the protection of their data.

Compliance

Blockchain technology can support regulatory compliance in the Middle East by streamlining the auditing and reporting processes. The transparent and tamper-proof nature of blockchain allows regulators to access and verify data more efficiently, reducing the need for manual audits and simplifying compliance efforts for organizations. However, compliance with data protection regulations, such as the European Union's General Data Protection Regulation (GDPR) or local data protection laws, can be challenging in a blockchain context. Issues surrounding the "right to be forgotten" and the permanent storage of personal data on blockchain networks can create conflicts with existing data protection laws. To address these concerns, organizations must carefully consider the design of their blockchain solutions, ensuring compliance with local and international regulations.

Blockchain and decentralized data management technologies offer significant opportunities for improving data governance in the Middle East. By leveraging the unique features of these technologies, organizations can enhance data privacy, security, and compliance. However, the adoption of blockchain and decentralized data management is not without challenges. To fully realize the potential of these technologies, organizations and governments in the Middle East must carefully navigate the complexities of privacy, security, and compliance, while investing in the development of the regional blockchain ecosystem and expertise.

Regional data governance initiatives and collaborations

Ongoing and future regional data governance initiatives and collaborations within the Middle East are poised to play a significant role in improving data management, privacy, and security across the region. These initiatives aim to strengthen the region's data governance landscape and enable sustainable economic growth by addressing current challenges and leveraging new technologies. This investigation will discuss the potential impact of these initiatives on regional stability and economic growth, focusing on key collaborations and projects.

Regional Data Protection Regulations and Harmonization

As data protection and privacy become increasingly important, Middle Eastern countries have started to develop and implement comprehensive data protection regulations. For instance, the United Arab Emirates (UAE) introduced the Data Protection Law, while Saudi Arabia has enacted the Personal Data Protection Law. These efforts indicate a regional move towards harmonizing data protection regulations, which could facilitate cross-border data flows and enhance regional cooperation. The harmonization of data protection regulations can lead to increased investor confidence, as it reduces the complexities associated with navigating different legal frameworks. By promoting a common standard for data governance, the region can attract international businesses and investments, fostering economic growth and regional stability.

Smart City Initiatives

Several Middle Eastern countries are investing heavily in smart city initiatives, which rely on effective data governance to optimize urban planning, resource allocation, and public services. For example, the UAE's Smart Dubai initiative aims to make Dubai the smartest and happiest city globally by leveraging technology and data-driven strategies. Similarly, Saudi Arabia's NEOM project, a planned cross-border city, aims to create a sustainable, data-driven urban environment. These smart city initiatives can significantly impact regional economic growth by fostering innovation, attracting investment, and creating new business opportunities. Effective data governance practices within these projects ensure data privacy and security, ultimately contributing to regional stability by bolstering trust in public and private sector institutions.

Regional Cybersecurity Collaborations

In response to growing cyber threats, Middle Eastern countries are increasingly collaborating on cybersecurity initiatives to enhance regional data security. The Gulf Cooperation Council (GCC) has established the GCC Cyber Security Center, which aims to facilitate cooperation among GCC member states on cybersecurity matters, share best practices, and develop regional cybersecurity capabilities.

By fostering collaboration and information sharing on cybersecurity, the Middle Eastern countries can better protect their critical infrastructure and sensitive data from cyberattacks. This, in turn, can promote regional stability by reducing the risk of conflicts arising from cyber threats and contribute to economic growth by ensuring the security of digital assets.

Capacity Building and Educational Initiatives

Recognizing the importance of skilled human resources in implementing effective data governance practices, Middle Eastern countries are investing in capacity building and educational initiatives. These efforts aim to develop a skilled workforce capable of managing, analyzing, and securing the region's vast amounts of data. For example, the UAE has established the Mohamed bin Zayed University of Artificial Intelligence (MBZUAI), which focuses on artificial intelligence and data science research and education.

Capacity building initiatives, such as the establishment of specialized universities and training programs, can contribute to economic growth by fostering a skilled workforce, which can drive innovation and attract international businesses seeking skilled professionals.

Cross-Border Data Sharing Agreements

To facilitate regional cooperation and development, Middle Eastern countries are exploring cross-border data sharing agreements. These agreements can enable collaboration in various sectors, such as healthcare, financial services, and law enforcement, and can contribute to regional stability by fostering trust and cooperation among countries. Cross-border data sharing agreements can also contribute to economic growth by promoting the seamless flow of information and enabling data-driven decision-making. However, it is crucial to ensure that these agreements adhere to data protection and privacy standards to maintain the trust of businesses and individuals.

Ongoing and future regional data governance initiatives and collaborations within the Middle East have the potential to significantly impact data management, privacy, and security across the region.

Vision for a data-empowered Middle East

A vision for the future of data governance in the Middle East is one that embraces innovation, collaboration, and responsible use of data. This vision can be achieved through technological advancements, regional cooperation, and the development of robust data governance frameworks and practices that empower individuals, businesses, and governments. By fostering a data-driven culture that prioritizes security, privacy, and compliance, the Middle East can unlock its potential as a global leader in data governance.

Technological Advancements

The Middle East can leverage emerging technologies, such as artificial intelligence (AI), machine learning, and blockchain, to revolutionize data governance practices. These technologies can enhance data management, privacy, and security, enabling businesses and governments to make data-driven decisions while ensuring the protection of sensitive information. AI and machine learning can help automate data governance tasks, such as data classification, data quality management, and anomaly detection, thus reducing the potential for human error and improving efficiency. Blockchain technology, with its decentralized and secure nature, can provide a tamper-proof and transparent framework for data management, ensuring data privacy and security. By adopting these technologies and fostering a culture of innovation, the Middle East can position itself at the forefront of the global data governance landscape.

Regional Cooperation

Regional cooperation is essential to achieving a harmonized data governance landscape in the Middle East. Countries in the region can work together to develop and adopt common data protection regulations, similar to the European Union's General Data Protection Regulation (GDPR). This harmonization can facilitate cross-border data flows and encourage collaboration among businesses and governments within the region. Moreover, regional cooperation can lead to the establishment of joint data-sharing agreements and data governance initiatives that promote economic growth, social development, and regional stability. By working together, Middle Eastern countries can tackle shared challenges and create synergies that benefit the entire region.

Robust Data Governance Frameworks and Practices

The development of robust data governance frameworks and practices is crucial for empowering individuals, businesses, and governments in the Middle East. This involves creating comprehensive data protection laws, establishing data governance bodies, and implementing best practices that align with global standards. These frameworks and practices should be designed to promote transparency, accountability, and data stewardship. By adopting clear guidelines and policies, businesses and governments can ensure data privacy, security, and compliance while promoting trust among stakeholders.

Empowerment of Individuals

The future of data governance in the Middle East should prioritize the empowerment of individuals by providing them with greater control over their data. This can be achieved by implementing data protection laws that grant individuals the right to access, correct, delete, and restrict the processing of their personal information. Furthermore, promoting digital literacy and data privacy awareness among citizens is essential to ensure that individuals understand their rights and the importance of responsible data sharing. By empowering individuals, the Middle East can foster a data-driven culture that values privacy and security.

Supporting Businesses

To achieve a future of innovative and responsible data governance in the Middle East, it is essential to support businesses in their data governance efforts. This includes providing access to resources, such as training programs, workshops, and expert guidance, to help businesses implement effective data governance practices. Furthermore, governments should incentivize businesses to adopt innovative technologies and data governance solutions by offering grants, tax breaks, and other financial incentives. By creating a supportive environment for businesses to invest in data governance, the Middle East can drive economic growth and innovation while ensuring data privacy and security.

Government Initiatives and Policies

Governments in the Middle East have a critical role to play in shaping the future of data governance in the region. They can do this by implementing policies that promote data protection and compliance, investing in infrastructure and technologies to support data governance, and fostering a culture of innovation and collaboration. Furthermore, governments should actively engage with international data governance organizations and participate in global dialogues on data protection and privacy. This involvement can help Middle Eastern countries stay abreast of the latest developments in data governance and ensure that their practices align with global standards.

Workforce Development and Education

The future of data governance in the Middle East depends on a skilled workforce capable of managing, analyzing, and securing the region's vast amounts of data. To achieve this, the region must invest in workforce development and education initiatives that focus on data governance, data science, and related fields. This includes establishing specialized universities, training programs, and research centers that foster talent and expertise in data governance. By nurturing a skilled workforce, the Middle East can drive innovation and attract international businesses seeking proficient professionals.

Public-Private Partnerships

Public-private partnerships (PPPs) can play a crucial role in achieving a future of innovative and responsible data governance in the Middle East. By collaborating on data governance initiatives, businesses and governments can pool resources, share best practices, and jointly tackle challenges. PPPs can facilitate the development and implementation of data governance frameworks, the adoption of innovative technologies, and the establishment of data governance bodies. Through these partnerships, the public and private sectors can work together to create a data governance ecosystem that benefits all stakeholders and fosters economic growth and regional stability.

Fostering a Data-Driven Culture

To fully realize the potential of data governance in the Middle East, it is essential to foster a data-driven culture that values data privacy, security, and compliance. This involves raising awareness about the importance of responsible data management among individuals, businesses, and governments. Efforts should be made to promote data literacy and educate stakeholders on the benefits of effective data governance, such as improved decision-making, reduced risk, and increased efficiency. By cultivating a data-driven culture, the Middle East can encourage the responsible use of data and ensure that data governance practices are deeply ingrained in the region's fabric.

Encouraging Innovation and Entrepreneurship

The Middle East should actively encourage innovation and entrepreneurship in the data governance space. This can be achieved by creating innovation hubs, incubators, and accelerators that focus on data governance and related technologies. By offering support, resources, and mentorship to startups and entrepreneurs working on data governance solutions, the Middle East can foster a vibrant ecosystem of innovation that drives progress in data management, privacy, and security.

The future of data governance in the Middle East hinges on embracing innovation, collaboration, and the responsible use of data. By leveraging technological advancements, fostering regional cooperation, and developing robust data governance frameworks and practices, the region can empower individuals, businesses, and governments to unlock the full potential of data governance. This vision, if realized, can contribute significantly to regional stability, economic growth, and the overall prosperity of the Middle East.

Part V

Concluding Reflections

Chapter 11

Reflecting on the Middle Eastern Digital Transformation

Conclusion

Key takeaways from the book

Based on the key takeaways from this book, the most critical aspects of data governance in the Middle East that are essential for its digital future can be summarized as follows:

1. *Regulatory environment:* The Middle East is experiencing rapid growth in the digital realm, necessitating the development of a robust regulatory environment that aligns with global best practices. Countries in the region need to continue enhancing their data protection laws and cybersecurity regulations to ensure data privacy and security for individuals, businesses, and governments. Adopting GDPR-like comprehensive data protection regulations will contribute significantly to creating a stable and secure digital ecosystem in the region.

2. *International data-sharing agreements:* As the Middle East becomes more connected globally, cross-border data flows and data sovereignty become increasingly relevant. Strengthening international data-sharing agreements and fostering regional cooperation in data

governance will be crucial for creating a seamless data-sharing environment that facilitates economic growth, innovation, and collaboration among countries in the region.

3. *Public and private sector involvement:* The public and private sectors play a vital role in shaping data governance practices. Governments must take the lead in developing policies and initiatives that promote data protection and compliance while creating an environment that encourages innovation. The private sector, on the other hand, must ensure that their data governance practices align with regional regulations and global standards, thereby protecting their customers' data and maintaining trust.

4. *Embracing technology:* Emerging technologies such as artificial intelligence, machine learning, blockchain, and decentralized data management have the potential to revolutionize data governance in the Middle East. By harnessing these technologies, the region can address challenges related to data privacy, security, and compliance, leading to a more transparent and efficient digital landscape.

5. *Industry-specific data governance:* Sectors like healthcare, finance, and smart cities require tailored data governance approaches that address their unique challenges and opportunities. By implementing successful data governance practices within these industries, the Middle East can enhance the quality of services, improve patient outcomes, ensure financial stability, and promote sustainable urban development.

6. *Collaboration and knowledge sharing:* The Middle East can learn from successful data governance implementations and best practices from around the world. By sharing knowledge and collaborating on initiatives, the region can develop innovative solutions to address its unique data governance challenges, fostering a culture of continuous improvement and growth.

7. *Future-oriented vision:* The Middle East's digital future will be shaped by its ability to create a comprehensive vision for data governance that embraces innovation, collaboration, and the responsible use of data. This vision must be supported by robust data governance frameworks and practices that empower individuals, businesses, and governments to harness the potential of the digital era while ensuring data privacy and security.

The Middle East's digital future depends on its ability to address the complex challenges of data governance effectively. By focusing on these critical aspects and fostering a culture of innovation, collaboration, and responsible data use, the region can unlock the full potential of the digital age and pave the way for a prosperous and secure future.

The role of data governance in shaping the Middle East's digital future

The role of data governance in shaping the Middle East's digital future is multifaceted and crucial. As the region embraces digital transformation and seeks to foster economic growth, effective data governance practices are integral to ensuring that the benefits of digitalization are maximized while the risks and challenges are mitigated. In this reflection, I will consider the role of technological advancements, regional cooperation, and data governance frameworks in shaping the Middle East's digital future.

Technological advancements are driving the digital revolution in the Middle East, with emerging technologies such as artificial intelligence (AI), machine learning, the Internet of Things (IoT), and blockchain transforming various sectors of the economy. These technologies generate massive amounts of data, which can offer valuable insights and drive innovation. However, the increasing complexity and scale of data management necessitate robust data governance practices that address privacy, security, and compliance concerns. Data governance will play a critical role in ensuring that the Middle East leverages the potential of these technologies responsibly and securely. Organizations in the region must implement data governance frameworks that not only address the unique challenges posed by these technologies but also facilitate their adoption and integration into existing systems. By prioritizing data privacy, security, and compliance, the region can harness the power of technological advancements while maintaining the trust of its citizens and fostering a stable digital ecosystem.

Regional cooperation is another essential aspect of the Middle East's digital future. Data governance practices can significantly benefit from collaboration and knowledge sharing among countries in the region. By working together, Middle Eastern countries can develop harmonized data protection laws and cybersecurity regulations that create a seamless and secure environment for cross-border data flows. Such regional cooperation can lead to the establishment of shared best practices, unified standards, and interoperable systems that promote innovation and facilitate economic growth. Moreover, regional cooperation can extend to the global level, with the Middle East participating in international data-sharing agreements and engaging in dialogue with other regions to learn from their experiences in data governance. The Middle East can benefit from adopting global standards, such as the European Union's General Data Protection Regulation (GDPR), which can enhance data protection and promote trust among individuals, businesses, and governments.

Data governance frameworks will play a pivotal role in shaping the Middle East's digital future. A comprehensive and robust framework that addresses the region's unique cultural, political, and legal landscape is necessary for successfully navigating the complexities of data governance in the Middle East. As the region evolves digitally, data governance frameworks must remain flexible and adaptable to accommodate emerging technologies and changing regulatory environments. These frameworks should prioritize the protection of personal data, ensure data security, and promote compliance with applicable laws and regulations. In addition to establishing robust frameworks, it is crucial for the Middle East to foster a culture of data governance that permeates both public and private sectors. This culture should emphasize the importance of data privacy, security, and compliance, as well as promote transparency and accountability in data management practices. To achieve this, governments should invest in education and training programs that equip individuals and organizations with the skills and knowledge required to implement effective data governance practices.

Furthermore, the region should encourage innovation and entrepreneurship in the field of data governance by supporting startups and businesses that develop cutting-edge data management solutions. By fostering a vibrant ecosystem of data governance innovators, the Middle East can position itself as a global leader in the digital era. Data governance will play a critical role in shaping the Middle East's digital future. To fully harness the potential of digital transformation and foster economic growth, the region must prioritize the development of robust data governance frameworks, promote regional and global cooperation, and invest in education and innovation. By embracing responsible and secure data management practices, the Middle East can pave the way for a prosperous digital future that benefits its citizens, businesses, and governments alike.

Final thoughts and recommendations for stakeholders

As a stakeholder in the Middle East's data governance landscape, my primary concerns and priorities can be broadly categorized into the following areas:

1. *Compliance with regional and international regulations:* Ensuring that businesses and organizations in the region adhere to the existing data protection laws and guidelines is of utmost importance. Compliance with regulatory requirements not only ensures data privacy and security but also helps establish trust between businesses, consumers, and governments.

2. *Data privacy and security:* Safeguarding the privacy and security of personal and sensitive data should be a priority for all stakeholders. This involves implementing robust data management practices, utilizing advanced security measures, and raising awareness about data privacy rights among citizens.

3. *Education and training:* Building a skilled workforce with a strong understanding of data governance principles and practices is essential for the region's digital future. Investing in education and training programs will help equip individuals and organizations with the necessary skills to navigate the complex data governance landscape.

4. *Encouraging innovation:* Fostering a culture of innovation and entrepreneurship in the field of data governance can position the Middle East as a global leader in this area. Supporting startups and businesses that develop cutting-edge data management solutions will help drive progress in data governance and contribute to the region's economic growth.

5. *Regional and global cooperation:* Collaborating with other countries and international organizations is crucial for developing and implementing effective data governance practices. Sharing knowledge, best practices, and resources can help the region address common challenges and work towards harmonized data governance frameworks.

6. *Prioritize data governance as a strategic imperative:* Recognizing the importance of data governance in the digital age is crucial for all stakeholders. Individuals, businesses, and governments should

prioritize data governance as a key component of their overall digital transformation efforts and allocate sufficient resources to support these initiatives.

7. *Foster collaboration and knowledge sharing:* Stakeholders across the Middle East should actively engage in knowledge sharing and collaboration to address common challenges and develop innovative solutions. Regional platforms, conferences, and workshops can provide valuable opportunities for stakeholders to share experiences, best practices, and lessons learned.

8. *Invest in capacity building and talent development:* Developing a skilled workforce with expertise in data governance is essential for the region's digital future. Governments, businesses, and educational institutions should invest in training programs, workshops, and certification courses to equip individuals with the necessary skills and knowledge to navigate the complex data governance landscape.

9. *Adopt a risk-based approach to data governance:* Given the rapidly evolving digital landscape, stakeholders should adopt a risk-based approach to data governance that balances innovation with data protection. This involves continuously assessing and mitigating potential risks associated with data collection, storage, and processing while promoting responsible data use.

10. *Leverage technology to enhance data governance practices:* As technology continues to advance, stakeholders should explore the potential of emerging technologies such as artificial intelligence, machine learning, and blockchain to improve data governance practices. These technologies can help streamline data management processes, enhance data privacy and security, and enable more efficient regulatory compliance.

11. *Develop and update robust legal and regulatory frameworks:* Governments in the Middle East should continually review and update their data protection laws and regulations to ensure they remain

relevant and effective in the face of emerging technologies and new data governance challenges. This includes aligning domestic legislation with global best practices and fostering cross-border collaboration to facilitate data sharing and cooperation.

12. *Promote transparency and trust:* Fostering trust among stakeholders is essential for the successful implementation of data governance initiatives. Transparency in data handling practices, along with clear communication and engagement with individuals, businesses, and other stakeholders, can help build confidence in the region's data governance ecosystem.

13. *Implement best practices and learn from successful case studies:* Stakeholders should strive to implement best practices and lessons learned from successful data governance initiatives in the Middle East and around the world. This includes adopting a holistic approach to data governance that encompasses data quality, privacy, security, and compliance.

14. *Encourage public-private partnerships:* Governments and businesses should work together to develop public-private partnerships that promote innovation, knowledge sharing, and capacity building in data governance. Such collaborations can help drive progress and create an enabling environment for responsible data management across the region.

15. *Keep an eye on the future:* As the digital landscape continues to evolve, stakeholders must remain agile and adaptive to new developments in data governance. By staying informed about emerging trends, challenges, and opportunities, individuals, businesses, and governments can ensure that their data governance practices remain relevant and effective in the years to come.

The future of data governance in the Middle East depends on the collective efforts of individuals, businesses, and governments to prioritize responsible data management, embrace collaboration, and invest in capacity building. By working together to address the challenges and seize the opportunities presented by the digital age, stakeholders can pave the way for a more secure, prosperous, and data-driven future in the region.

About the Author

Dr. Tosin Ekundayo is a luminary in the expansive world of data governance and a passionate advocate for open data initiatives, particularly within emerging economies. Holding a distinguished degree from Synergy University, Dr. Ekundayo's expertise is deep-rooted in the intricate weave of technology, governance, and sustainable development.

His focus on the Middle East is not coincidental; it's the result of years of immersive research, collaborations with regional stakeholders, and a profound understanding of the cultural and technological nuances that define the region. Dr. Ekundayo's work, spanning the African continent to the heart of the Arabian desert, continually unravels the dynamic intersections where tradition meets innovation.

A sought-after speaker on the global stage, he has been instrumental in shaping policy and practice in the digital data realm. His insights, drawn from rigorous fieldwork and analytical studies, have earned him accolades and respect among peers and policymakers alike.

"Desert Data" is more than just a book; it's a synthesis of Dr. Ekundayo's dedication to promoting equitable data access and an exploration of the transformative potential of well-governed data in a region on the cusp of a digital renaissance. Dive in to embark on a journey with a guide whose vision and knowledge are truly unparalleled.